cursed blessings/blessed curses

cursed blessings/blessed curses
poetic tantrums & written observations

robert l. darden

Writers Club Press
San Jose New York Lincoln Shanghai

cursed blessings/blessed curses
poetic tantrums & written observations

All Rights Reserved © 2001 by Robert L. Darden

No part of this book may be reproduced or transmitted in any form or by any means, graphic, electronic, or mechanical, including photocopying, recording, taping, or by any information storage retrieval system, without the permission in writing from the publisher.

Writers Club Press
an imprint of iUniverse.com, Inc.

For information address:
iUniverse.com, Inc.
5220 S 16th, Ste. 200
Lincoln, NE 68512
www.iuniverse.com

ISBN: 0-595-19086-3

Printed in the United States of America

*for selina white,
the truest and most free spirit
that i've ever known;*

*for everyone who has ever felt the need
to challenge their surroundings;*

*for my husband, anthony r. fox,
without whom this would never have come to be;*

*for all my gay and lesbian
brothers and sisters:*

*our time is now,
our lives are eternal…*

Contents

doubt/no doubt. 1
self-portrait. 2
defiance delivered 3
"how's it goin', big guy?" 4
…the hand that feeds you. 6
adventurously apathetic yet tumultuously calm. 7
the drums. 8
cuidado/achtung! 9
anger. 10
Wohir komen Sie? 11
why should i believe? 12
(untitled) 13
what you see… 14
all dressed down and no one to upset. 15
to be continued. 16
titlesong. 18
baby.boy. 20
victim(…). 21
angst. 22
yesterday. 23
my own contagion. 24
resist not evil. [in memory and defense of matthew] 25
i, of sound mind… 26
…descending. 27
so what? 28
priorities. 30
a bump in the road to love… 31
emotional erosion. 32
blacksheep. 33
tears… 34

indifference.	35
(untitled…)	36
the beauty riddle.	37
halfslumbre.	38
in the dark.	39
inside of me.	40
rhetorical doubt.	41
buried treasure.	42
th' ballad of th' confused one…	43
not a damn t'give…	44
my heart in my hand.	45
unlabeled rage.	46
waiting.	47
life: III-1/2.	48
fortune cookies.	49
emergence…	50
th' bottom line.	51
the flight of the black dove.	52
allow me to ramble: part one~love(?)	54
misjudgment day.	56
ascension incognito.	58
progression?	60
the cost of global unity.	62
the upper hand.	63
should've.	64
a lover's test…	66
future in flames.	67
androgyny.	68
homogenous.	69
human unity.	70
pleasure.	71
the essence of a destiny unknown.	72

karma.	73
seasons of sorrow (I-IV).	74
the value of friendship.	75
censorship: a realist's p.o.v.	76
cogitations.	77
disillusional dismay.	78
wishful thinking.	79
wishful thinking: part 2.	80
III~ii~I (three-to-one).	81
things have always been this way…	82
dining on unity.	83
the frantic cycle./the fear of being fearless.	84
overcome…	85
would you…?	86
my man and his way…	88
reflections, in the key of me minor: part 1.	89
to be legendary.	91
how long?…	92
indulgencia.	93
outside.	94
masquerade.	95
forbidden tongue.	96
to have and have not.	97
2001:begin anew.	99
wrong from the start.	100
lovelust.	101
the power/your eyes.	102
how?	103
the hunger.	104
apology not offered.	106
an observation…	107
innocence.	108

cursed blessings/blessed curses

soliloquy.	109
untitled…	110
blackness looking back at me…	111
tired.	112
an annoyance.	113
an annoyance: updated/rethought.	114
allow me you…	115
a message to my people….	117
homo sects, you all.	119
shadows.	121
face of the enemy.	122
ease my pain.	124
to know love…	125
the need…	126
misled you.	127
when me met. [for my husband]	128
from nothing to something…	129
beautiful beaste.	131
acknowledgment.	132
the other side…	134
shades…	136
all and nothing…	138
m.perfection.	139
twenty-four double-negative.	140
on the real.	142
fast forward.	144
negative~positivity.	145
as forever unbalanced…	146
doomchildren.	148
peace: my prayer.	149
you should know…	150

the quintessential acquired taste of a bone dipped in chocolate: a sexcapade…	152
good night pooh-bear, love piglet.	154
hallucinations.	160
shattered equilibrium.	161
darkness.	162
the perseverance of doubt.	163
a moment of regret.	164
bitter…	165
on the road to insanity…	166
storm.	167
if it's me that you see…	168
cette homme…	170
mosaique.	172
deux hommes.	173
symphonique.	174
zero.	175
harmony.	176
dragphuck!!!	177
bondage (light).	178
bondage (severe).	179
revolver.	181
the sadist and the masochist.	182
ego-trip (harsh/crude).	183
crowded solitaire.	184
ma facade.	185
pain.	186
requiem d'amour?	187
seeing that you do not know me…	188
je suis voici!	189
a chance for change.	190
hug.	191

cursed blessings/blessed curses

cast away your thoughts of loving me. 192
cocky misguidance. 193
j/k/m/a. 194
oblivion. 195
je m'en fous! 196
love '95. 197
me times i. 198
aural copulation. 199
le jeu d'amour. 200
breakup!! 201
in summary… 202
everything. 203

Preface

I have love in me, the likes of which you can scarce imagine, and rage the likes of which you can not believe. If I can not satisfy one I shall indulge the other...

———Mary Shelley

This is a collection of writings which began as a sort of self-therapy when I was around the age of 14, maybe 15. I started writing due to the fact that I didn't feel that I had anyone that I could talk to, for various reasons, mostly being that I didn't trust most of the people in my immediate presence. I realized that by putting pen to paper, I could "deal with" all the problems that I was encountering. I later realized that by not talking about the things that were bothering me, I was actually creating more problems for myself, but of course, this just gave me more to write about!

I then learned that I could write about things other than myself, but I remained my favorite topic, and I knew more about me than I did anything else, even though that lack of knowledge about self was pretty much what led to my writing.

Over the years, my interests grew from just my lack of trust for others, to all sorts of other arenas, mostly of a sexual nature, due to the fact that I was even further into my deviant dalliances than I was when I began writing. I acknowledged that I had a really dark, deep, and serious sexuality that most people either could not or would not try to understand, which was completely OK with me, because I figured the less time I spent talking about it, the more time I had to add episodes to it...

And in time, my adventures and excursions grew, affording me more of a position of a "loner" somewhat, which allowed me to observe others. I took the things that I witnessed and put them on paper. Those situations, along

cursed blessings/blessed curses

with all the others, are what you have here, on paper. Some of them are a little dark, some are hopeful, and some are downright scary, but I have nothing to hide. I hope that some of you can get something out of these words, because I know how much they have meant, and still mean, to me. I know what it's like to suffer in silence, I know what it's like to suffer out loud, and I know what it's like to just want it all to end. But I also know exactly what it's like to want to do something about my surroundings, and it has been said that knowing is half the battle. By putting my thoughts down on paper, I can always look back on them and see just how much I've grown since the time that I actually wrote those words for the first time. It can be frightening to look back on those times, but it's better than not being able to look back at all…

Even though there are some dark moments here, there are some bursts of sunshine also, and I've tossed in some elements of pride as well. Interpret them as you will…

doubt/no doubt.

i have absolutely no doubt
who i am,
although there is tremendous doubt
surrounding where i came from.
i doubt that there was any
concern involved, ever.
i doubt that there was any
love involved, during.
i don't doubt that there was
remorse involved, afterward.
there is severe doubt
that i will ever "get past it",
and although i know that i should
just let it go,
i doubt that it will ever happen.

sometimes i doubt that i have
any justifiable reason to doubt
all the things of which i am not sure,
but, as they say:
"when in doubt…"

self-portrait.

ineffectual intellectual.
charismatic; over-sexual.
enigmatic *and* ineffable:
obviously acceptable.
self-aware, not self-complacent.
self-designed through own arrangement.
self-sufficient with bursts of greatness.
self-assured and sometimes fragrant.
free to care, but not to flaunt it.
free to love, yet not to want it.

i'm a man of many moods,
i'm a man of much passion.
i create my own styles,
i dictate my own fashion.

defiance delivered

(o.k., go ahead…)
seize this moment, take it from me.
put me down as you try to become me.
talk about me, dis me, snub me,
then turn around and try to love me…

pour your poison. talk your trash.
try to make me kiss your ass.
enjoy your time in higher-class,
but realize—this, too, will pass…

redefine me. try to change me.
disconnect and rearrange me.
find a new way to contain me,
but know that you will never chain me…

pour your poison. talk your trash.
try to make me kiss your ass.
enjoy your time in higher-class,
but realize—this, too, will pass…

"how's it goin', big guy?"

…i have the cursed blessing/blessed curse of being what is known as a "big guy". i am 6'2" tall, and i weigh approximately 250 lbs. i am, pretty much, built like the football player that i *used* to be. i say that this is a blessing because, being a "big guy", most people don't feel the need to fuck with me. they just let me go on and be me, doing what i wanna do, when i wanna do it, how i wanna do it. but, i consider it also a curse. for some reason, people feel that since i *look* like a football player that i should *be* a football player, or worse, they think that i should give a damn about football. i always get questions about this game or that game, and this team or that team. some people even go as far as asking if i am a football player. they want to know who i play for. when they find out that i don't play football, they reinforce the fact that i look like a football player. like i've gone through one second of my day not knowing that i am as big as i am. but i guess that since they feel so strongly that i look like a football player, that i must have the stereotypical mentality of a football player, and therefore i can't even think for myself? could that be it?

first of all, i don't get why people just can't accept a person's looks without feeling that they are entitled to give commentary on said look, especially when the possessor of that look is over twice the size of the possessors of those 'misrepresented compliments'. second, how about the fact that nine-times-out-of-ten, i get asked "the question" at my place of employ: "yes, i *am* a football player, which is why i am standing behind a counter taking your lunch order. would you like a medium or a large soda with that?"

third, exactly how comfortable can a person get with a complete stranger? do you just look at someone, decide that they look a certain way, and then, after 15 seconds with them, just start asking mundane, personal questions based on their appearance in your eyes? is this how ice is broken these days? would you just walk up to an 'obviously' pregnant woman and start talking about how much childbirth has changed over the years, just assuming that because she is with child, she knows all there is to know about the subject? you know, even if she does, do you think she really wants to talk about it? with someone whom she doesn't even know? and should you actually believe that you're the only person on the face of the earth that has noticed her condition? go ahead, just ask her if you could rub her belly. and here's a thought—what if she's not actually pregnant? how embarrassing would *that* be? to you and to her. i know for a fact that it happens. a friend of mine asked a co-worker of hers (whom she didn't really know that well to begin with) how her new baby was doing. the co-worker replied that she did not have any children. my friend felt the uncontrollable need to stick her foot further into her mouth and said, "but weren't you pregnant just a little while back?"

which caused this snap-back: "no! i was not! and i never have been!"

touche'!

i guess the point that i am half-attempting to make is that you really shouldn't make verbal commentary to go along with the unsolicited assumptions you made after seeing a person and not knowing any actual facts about that person…

thanx.

...the hand that feeds you.

i've always been told
to not bite the hand
that feeds me.
i feel, however, that
there are times when
it is o.k. to bite the
hand that feeds you.
if that hand is trying
to feed you something that
you do not wish to eat,
bite it. (hard.)
if that hand appears to be
a little less clean
than you would prefer,
bite it. (carefully.)
if you do not wish to
be fed by that hand,
bite it. (twice.)
after all, are you not
capable of feeding yourself?
or is it just that you are so
completely dependent upon
someone else to get the
nourishment that you need
that you allow others to
put themselves in your face
on a continual basis?
fuck that!
if i am not capable of
getting my own,
i do not deserve that
of anyone else...

adventurously apathetic yet tumultuously calm.

chaos is all that makes sense any more;
if it ain't all fucked up, then what's it here for?
the days have no nights while the nights have
    no ends.
the prospect of being killed relies on old friends.

the drums.

moving to the beats of so many different
    drummers,
sometimes it appears that i'm just standing
    still…

cuidado/achtung!

just because i welcome you
does not mean that
i'll be your mat…

anger.

there's a great deal of anger within me,
and even though approximately 99% of it
is purely justified, just to know that i have
all of this anger terrifies me. sometimes.
sometimes, it just makes me angry…

Wohir komen Sie?

you don't think i know
where i'm coming from.
but that's not what bothers you,
is it?
the fact that you don't think
that i know means that
you don't know where i'm
coming from, doesn't it?
what should really bother you,
however, is this:
i know exactly where i'm coming from…

why should i believe?

forgive me but i do believe
that it seems that
your god made a mistake.
in fact, i believe that he
may have made more than one.
how so, you ask?
well, for one,
if you were made in his image,
with him being
omnipotent (supposedly)
and all-caring,
then how can it be that you
(though you know me not)
hate me so?
if you are his child,
filled with the same compassion
that (supposedly) he represents,
how can you disregard me
so quickly
having no actual knowledge
of what i'm about or
or who th'hell i really am?
you claim that your god is righteous,
and that he is the way and the truth and the light,
and that he is the only answer
to all questions regardless of source:
ok, question—
if your god is all that, then
why would he have created
something as unwanted,
unloved, and unprepared for
as i…

(untitled)

you have your freedoms; you have your dreams;
you have your wishes: are they now what they
    seemed?
of the things which you wanted, of the things
    which you craved,
of the things you did covet—none will go to
    your grave.

what you see…

with me, what you see is all that you get,
but you haven't seen all there is to see yet.
you see only a big, brown man with no hair,
and you've never imagined there could be
    more there.

i am more than my skin, so much more than
    my tone;
could you dare to recognize what to you is
    unknown?
if you just took the time, you would see all
    that's there,
but 'til you open your mind, your vision rests
    impaired.

all dressed down and no one to upset.

...although it is no longer uncommon for a black man to possess intelligence, it appears that there is a certain way that an intelligent black man should present himself. i guess that would explain why it is such a shock to see a bald-headed, pierced, tatto'd black man with a "football player's build" perusing a book that has absolutely nothing to do with sports. i say "perusing" because one could never actually begin to believe that someone who fits said description could actually be "reading" the book, now could one?

so i guess as long as he is going to wear expensive suits, flashy, designer shoes, and pretty, silk ties (all sold to him by men dressed in the same manner), and he carries his books and things in an expensive, leather briefcase, he can read whatever he damn well pleases. but apparently, jeans and a t-shirt, sometimes even khakis, are not to be considered "proper reading attire" for "today's black man".

newsflash: i have earned the right to possess this intelligence, and i will carry it in any muthafuckin' package i choose!!!

thanx.

to be continued.

a boy.
created.
not intended.
born anyway.
surrendered to people
who knew
nothing about him,
or anyone like him.
unprepared.
undesired.
unamused.
thought himself
better than
all those around him:
hard to feel bad
about feeling that way
when time after time
they proved him to be right.
never asked to be created.
never asked to be born.
never asked to be a burden.
regardless,
all three occured.
all three being
no design of his own.
removed himself from
that horrid equation.
got up. got out. got his own.
got real. got a grip. got over it.
couldn't stay there another minute.
sorry, no apologies.

robert l. darden

gotta be movin' on:
to be continued…

a storm,
which takes place
where the mind
should reside,
causes words to rain down,
leaving their staining splashes
on the paper.
lightning strikes
and another failure
is illuminated
for all to recognize
within the shadows
of all the failures of the past.
the winds of anger and confusion
cause those words to flutter around,
forming rant-like sentence fragments
and random admissions to
gush forth,
the gusts and gales
of laughter
permeate the soul
and prayers for the end are begun:
to be continued…

titlesong.

...to be wanted. that's all most people ever need, and most of them, eventually get it. it may or may not be by the person or persons whom *they* want, but they are, inevitably wanted. i, too, am wanted, wanted by the person whom i actually want to want me, and as love would have it, i want him, too. however, having never been like most other people, i have another need, one that, apparently, understandably, will never be reconciled. i have the need to have been created in, by, and because of love. twenty-eight years have transpired and the person who was supposed to have been the most important figure in my life can not even simply admit to the fact that she contributed nothing to my creation. how am i supposed to have any relationship with someone who can not, will not, be honest with me about the most vital of information that i desire and require? being the stubborn, "self-made" man that i have become, i refuse to ask for this information, even though i'm sure most would argue that this would be the easiest, fastest, and best way to obtain that knowledge. i have reasons for not asking outright, the most blatant to myself is this: i'm sure that i would be lied to. if they have not come up off of this information voluntarily, not even once in 28 years, why would they just automatically answer a question simply because i ask it? in fact, through no devices of my own, i've already been flat out lied to about this exact same question that i refuse to ask...

    i guess the point i am trying to make is this: there are situations that i refer to as "cursed blessings", and there are other situations that i call "blessed curses". a "cursed blessing" is, essentially, when something beautiful and pure is born of intentions that were not well thought-out or pure to begin with, usually bred through ignorance. a "blessed curse" is when something that causes grief and heartache actually carries the potential to make the bearer a stronger, better person in spite of the ignorance which spawned it. i feel that my conception, birth, and (eventual) adoption are, simultaneously, cursed blessings and blessed curses. i never asked to be created. i never asked to be born. i would never have asked to have been adopted (especially by the people who *did* adopt me). but, if none of the aforementioned had happened, i would not be here, the strong, able-bodied, sharp-minded, defiantly individual, dark-

robert l. darden

humoured young man putting these words to paper. i would not be in love with one of the most amazing men on the face of this planet. i would not have the emotional and creative ranges that allow me to listen to rock, rap, classical, country, and pop/r&b with the same amount of interest, nor would i be able to sit down and have intellectual stimulation with anyone i choose. cursed blessings/blessed curses…

baby.boy.

babyboy was created
before babyboy was intended.
there were times babyboy wished
his beginning had been ended.
but babyboy has transitioned,
now a grown-ass man.
not a child anymore,
on "his own two" he stands.
once babyboy was foolish,
believed all he was told:
those foolish days have ended,
babyboy's too damn old.

victim(...).

you let them call you all those names.
you went along while they played their games.
you sat and did nothing while they offered abuse,
but to claim that you suffered, then you must
    be confused.

they taunted and teased you from the beginning,
yet you just sat there. silently. grinning.
the heartache you felt came through your own
    hand,
for you had not the courage on your own feet
    to stand,

so, no, my dear, you ain't a victim.
your feet weren't broken, you could've kicked 'em.
you could've turned and walked away,
but your silly ass decided just to stay...

angst.

your words can cause twice as much pain as a fist;
the punch i can't see, i can not resist.
my name is a curse when on your voice it rides;
upon sensing your presence, my confidence hides.
the bruises you cause won't be found on my skin,
but your pain makes its presence known deep
    down within.
the mask which i usually wear is my shield
which keeps all of my secrets from being revealed.
each step that i take leads me to the same place:
alone in a crowd, as defeat wears my face.
i can't stand on my own while i stand on your
    floor,
but without your assistance, i can't find the door.
your words can cut deeper than the slice of a
    knife—
accepting your love means denouncing my life…

yesterday.

yesterday was the last day i'd look at myself
and have no idea of what i see,
for today is the day that i tune out all else—
each day from today, the focus is me.

the time that i've spent making everyone love me
is time that i should've spent loving myself,
so it's time i devote some of my time to me—
from this moment on, fuck the rest.

i've played all the games and've grown tired of
    the players,
a true friend among them i have yet to find,
and the friends i have known don't make my
    house a home,
'cause they simply can't deal with my mind…

my own contagion.

i believe that i may be my very own contagion:
i've made myself sick on more than one occasion,
then cleansed my dead skin to the point of
    abrasion,
but in removing the sickness, i removed the
    sensation.

my fear of being fearless has attacked me again:
the sickness i sense is no longer within.
as the old nears completion, the new shall begin,
but i'm not sure which one will re-build my skin.

i sit in the dark so my flesh i can't see,
all the while i still feel all the sickness that's me.
sometimes i sit wondering why it all has to be
'til my voices yell "shut-up!", and i'm forced to
    agree…

resist not evil. [in memory and defense of matthew]

...if you kill me because of what i believe,
then you prove me right,
and therefore, i die in glory...

what is it about you that discomforts you so,
that you have to attack all that you do not know?
does the fact that you don't know why i do what
    i do
make you fear that i'll next wish to do it to you?
do you think of this often, yet you just won't admit
that your fears and your fantasies are the same
    damn bullshit?
just the fact that i am everything that i be
makes your awareness of self hate everything
    that's like me.
if i say what i think and/or say what i feel,
then i've said too damn much, but i said what
    was real.
i don't cause your unrest, i can't cause your unease,
but you think that i do—could you tell me
    how, please?
i be flesh. i be blood. i be bone. just like you.
i just live my life different: i live my life true...

i, of sound mind…

do you see me?
i stand here before you
a proud, capable, young,
black,
homosexual
man.
individual. independent. in control.
my beliefs may not be yours.
my ideals may not be yours.
my goals may not be yours.
fine, for i myself am not yours.
i belong to me.
no one else.
the life that i live
shall be lived
in the manner which i choose to live it.
i am entitled to this right,
and like you, i'm entitled to
many more.
you have the right to
agree or disagree with me.
you have the right to
become angry with me.
you have the right to love me.
you have the right to hate me.
you have the right to choose me as either
your friend or your foe;
whatever choice you make,
my life goes on.
with or without you.
with me in command.
so, tell me now:
do you see me?

...descending.

promises made. promises broken.
promises carried on words never spoken.
the light from your eyes, like a fire in the dark.
the tears from my eyes put an end to that spark.
can you hear how i feel by the sound of my voice?
can't you look and believe that i had no real choice?

i'm far too flamboyant your friend to be,
yet when it's all about favors, you call upon me.
to my face, i'm the greatest. no wrong can i do;
when my back turns, it seems pain is all i bring
        you...

you hide in shame,
conceal your fame,
yet everybody knows your name.
don't play that game,
it's you i blame:
i do not think i need explain.

you think you know me so damned well.
you think my secrets you can sell.
you think i should give you half a chance,
but you don't stand a chance in hell.

so what?

you don't look like me
you don't act like me
you don't smell like me
you don't fuck like me
you are not me
i am not you
we are not the same—
so what?

i don't know your name
i don't know your age
i don't know your story
i don't know your pain
i haven't lived your life
you haven't lived mine
we haven't lived the same—
so what?

we are not the same tone
we are not the same shape
we are not the same blood
we are not the same race
i don't think like you
you don't think like me
we do not agree—
so what?

you don't know where i've been
i don't know where you're going
i don't know what you know
but i don't mind not knowing

robert l. darden

we don't dance the same dance
we don't sing the same song
we don't play the same game
(so) we can't get along?

we don't wear the same clothes
we don't eat the same food
though we breathe the same air
we're not in the same mood

i don't get what you're saying
you don't get me at all
but if we don't get together
then we're both gonna fall

i see you
and you see me
we both see that we're different—
so what?

priorities.

the odd, intoxicating aroma
of stale bread
molests the nostrils
of a man who knows not
the taste of bread in any form.
tempting as it may be,
he goes on in the manner
in which he was doing
before he was so rudely
interrupted by the smell…

a bump in the road to love…

how do you let go of memories
that aren't even your own,
yet you can see them so vividly
that they chill you to the bone?
how do you begin to attempt to forget
the face of a man you've never known,
when the man with whom you'd share a life
used to welcome that face home?
how do you establish trust
when you can't even trust yourself?
how can you convince the man you love
that it's only him and no one else?
how do you respond to questions
that he asks only of himself?
why should he respond to questions
that you won't answer your own damn self?

…presently, i'm torn between
what i can not see and who i did not know:
how can the future even half-way begin
when the past won't let the present go?

emotional erosion.

...echoing the sound of the rudely slammed door,
the lion inside lets out a fierce roar...

gazing out window while sitting in chair,
carelessly running fingers through hair.
thinking of moments, now past, yet so near:
feeling too weak to give in to fear.
wanting to cry but denying the need;
needing to share but too full of greed...
declaring stability (while falling apart),
pleading to end (knowing not how to start).
hearing strange voices from deep, deep within,
pushing them out as they creep right back in...
searching for methods to lock them away;
finding no utterance decent to say.
rising and moving away from the chair,
breaking the silence—screaming into thin air.
falling, quite suddenly, back down to the floor,
finding no power to do any more.

...staring at ceiling while lying on floor,
the lion inside—no more does it roar...

blacksheep.

having been exposed to only the love of his
    mother,
blacksheep yearned for the love of another.
dismissed by his own for not being a "brother",
he prayed for acceptance in this, that, or the
    other…

though he usually had less,
blacksheep always gave more:
he vowed that he'd find
the love he longed for…

he traveled the world in search of "the prize";
he found only cold hearts hidden behind lying
    eyes.
throughout his quest, he grew more and more
    wise—
but he still sleeps alone, and he constantly
    sighs…

even if he has less,
blacksheep will always give more,
and someday he'll find
the love he longs for…

tears...

being all that you are, can you be who you be?
knowing all that you know, do you know if
    you're free?
having seen what you've seen, do you claim to
    believe?
having felt all you've felt, do you feel you should
    grieve?
having spent all your time running wild in the
    sun,
do you feel you should stop, or continue to run?
with a song in your heart, do you feel you
    should sing?
can you welcome the joy your existence should
    bring?
when you open your eyes, do you see all that's
    there?
when presented with knowledge, do you take
    time to share?
as you stand on your own, do you look out for
    others?
as the pictures develop, do you see all the
    colours?
while the day fades to night, does the darkness
    bring fear?
as the dark turns to light, does the fear reappear?

...more tears are shed over answered prayers,
but tears still come to those who never get
    theirs...

indifference.

an iridescent sacrilege which causes me to ponder:
which way throughout this pilgrimage will my
    emotions wander?
complacency or aggravation, surely one will be my
    captor;
indifference is the salutation i'm greeted with
    thereafter…

while noticing the emptiness which fills my new
    surroundings,
my face wears a contentedness although my head is
    pounding.
my ignorance has shunned its bliss in search of new
    beginning;
indifference is now the kiss which smiles because he's
    winning.

a symphony of silence sets the tone for this embrace,
as a passive turn at violence leads a hand across my
    face.
my desire to retaliate begins to make me shiver.
my self-control eradicates—my tears now form a river.

a screaming burst of iridescence knocks me to my
    knees,
while indifference and effervescence engulf me in their
    breeze…

(untitled...)

raise your children,
    don't just raise your fists.
the faces you've punched
    you might should have kissed.
when you leave this place,
    do you think you'll be missed?
will the world as you knew it
    cease to exist?
have you done anything
    that you thought you would do?
can anything substantial
    be attributed to you?
have you caused any dreams,
    not your own, to come true?
have you dreamed any dreams
    that do not involve you?
is your mind focused on
    the one thing you can't see?
or do you not believe
    'till it begins to be?
do your heart and your mouth
    almost never agree,
while your mind paints it black
    so that neither can be?

the beauty riddle.

if you surround yourself with beautiful people,
how, then, do *you* rate?
do you stand out
    (because you're not as beautiful)?
do you blend
    (because you're equally beautiful)?
they say it's only skin deep,
but who's got that much skin?

halfslumbre.

you appear in my dream and i feel i must scream,
    as your face overwhelms and disturbs.
if i let you come in, will we fuck or be friends,
    and with either who knows what occurs?
is it heartbeat i hear, or the echoes of fear?
    perhaps it's just overhead thunder…
as i dance in the dark, my own fear lights a spark,
    so i stop and stand still—and just wonder.
your words fly by my ears, their breeze freezes
    my tears. i look into your eyes as i stumble:
the defenses i've built get entrapped by my guilt,
    and the walls, all around me, they
    crumble…
ensconced by desire which ignites my own fire,
    and it's your hand that tends to the flame.
then as sleep pulls me under, in your arms, i
    greet slumber, as i smile and repeat your
    sweet name…

in the dark.

i did not decide to dwell in your presence, but
        you can not seem to get past my past.
my hands aren't in either one of your pockets, so
        why is your head so damn far up my ass?
it seems to me that you dwell too long on what i
        do, or wear, or say.
you flash your bright smile, though it's clear all
        the while you loathe, hate, and fear me
        because i am gay.
you claim that i chose to live this life, so therefore,
        i've brought upon all my own pain.
but reality states that it's not choice, but fate, that
        keeps me from being overwhelmingly plain.
you carefully choose your every word so that
        your bigotry i won't detect,
but you sit and you stir, and it's you who's
        unnerved when your tactics don't give the
        desired effect.
i go on with my life, disregarding your evil,
        your character-impugning and
        thoughtless remarks.
though it's i who resides where your light does not
        shine, it's you who sits all alone in the dark.

inside of me.

i want to feel you
inside of me.
i want you to feel me,
inside and out.
i want you to feel
the places i come from:
i want you to know
what this feeling's about.

i need to feel you
inside of me.
i need to feel you,
touching my soul.
i need you to touch me
with all of your body;
naked, before you,
i give you control.

i can still feel you
inside of me.
you made quite an impression—
you touched me so deep.
i hunger and long for
our next time together,
but 'til i again see you,
these feelings i'll keep…
(…contemplating your body, contented i
 sleep…)

rhetorical doubt.

a voice (which knows not its owner)
repeatedly whispers my name.
do i answer it? if i ignore it,
will it go away? if i respond to it,
will it only continue to do what it does?
what do i have to lose (but my sanity)?
i shall ponder this over a cool drink of water…

buried treasure.

not a sight of perfection,
but beautiful still.
a heart full of promise,
yet lacking the will,
a soul to reach out to,
that soul just grows old,
for the mind wants to go there,
but the flesh is not bold.
the thoughts that keep coming back
now and again,
are suppressed by the fear
of going beyond "friend".
the eyes tell the secrets,
but can not break the shell
'round the one who falls not
for the one who has fell…

th' ballad of th' confused one...

    thoughts of suicide enter his mind at least three
        times a day,
    but he's too weak to carry 'em through, so those
        thoughts get push'd away.
    wond'rin how to "classiphy" is th' 2nd highest
        mental lapse:
    to go this way, or go the other, or maybe to go
        both, perhaps.
    th' next in th' line of most popular thoughts
        concerns th' ones he's lost:
    he's got no clue as to how to move on, even tho'
        he's paid th' cost.
    he worries that he may worry too much, but
        how can this be resolved?
    while thinkin' about it, he worries some mo', and
        just adds to his troubled cause.
    to give it all up would be too easy, but he really
        doesn't want to fight,
    so what can he do, but go to bed (for yet another
        sleepless night...).

not a damn t'give...

i got not a damn t'give
i got not a care t'share
done cried so many, many tears
my tear-maker done gone bare
who th'hell are they t'judge me
why th'fuck they feel th'need
they got nothin' else t'do
'cept cut me open 'n watch me bleed
they don't think my blood's like theirs
they don't think my tears are real
they don't think i got a heart so
they don't think that i can feel
i got dreams that got no endin's
i got stories can't be told
got no money but that don't matter
'cause all th'good shit done been sold
can't say th'things i wanna say
wouldn't be proper not out loud
can't stand out an' be myself
but don't like bein' with th'crowd
life's half over (so they tell me)
but i ain't even begun t'live
i (still) got not a care t'share
(an' still) got not a damn t'give

my heart in my hand.

my emotions are
ice cubes.
frozen blocks of water
which, at any moment,
could begin to boil,
yet their steam would
instantly return to ice.
my face wears a smile.
my hand clutches my own heart;
though it beats in my hand,
it still throbs within my chest.
a tear trickles past
my smiling lips,
and i begin to sing lyrics
to the songs barreling
through my head.
i know not why i feel
the way i do,
for i know not how i feel.
it's clear to me what i
should feel,
but the heart in my hand
is now as cold
as the ice cubes
which sit in a puddle
of my own tears…

unlabeled rage.

just because you took me in
does not mean that you own me.
your task was to guide and nurture me,
but tell me what you've shown me.
the love you claim you gave to me
was given through obligation :
you want to appear more than you are—
that's *my* interpretation.
if my respect is what you're seeking,
a long way you must go.
a genuine love or trust from me
i am sure you will never know.
the claim you offer that you're on my side
is evidence unadmissable,
therefore, in return, i offer you this :
my ass, for you, is kissable…

waiting.

i sit around waiting.
i no longer go
out with my friends.
all because i'm sitting waiting.
waiting for something
which i can neither commit to
nor ask to commit to me…
i wait because i'm an
ineffably insecure, hopeless fool.
and even though
i know this,
i'll continue to be found here.
waiting.
patience is about all i've got left.

life: III-1/2.

i've got no one to talk to, so i look up to the sky;
i feel so bad that i can't see—so weak that i
    can't cry.
i've got so many problems, and i don't even
    know why.
i wish i were in heaven, but i'm afraid to fly…

i found a few of the answers, but i know i still
    need more,
to know exactly what i'm doing and what i'm
    really looking for.
until then i guess i'll be here, sitting on this
    dirty floor:
i see the signs which lead to 'exit', but i've no
    keys for that door…

yesterday i heard voices—i don't remember what
    they said.
and though today, they've gone away, i can't get
    them out of my head.
breezes flow beneath my nose, carrying the smell
    of moulded bread.
usually, i see all colours—today, i see only red…

…i've got no one to talk to, so i look up to the sky;
i wish i were in heaven, but i'm afraid to fly…

fortune cookies.

the life that you live must be a life of your own.
be true to yourself, or be lost and alone.
information you don't possess
is the object that keeps you from being your best.
to set out for battle without the right tools
is to journey right into the valley of fools.
at present your future is held in your hands,
but you can't hold on, meeting others'
      demands…
find the courage within to do what you feel—
what others believe is not part of the deal.
acknowledge your power, establish your place,
and go into each day with a smile on your face.

emergence...

it is fairly difficult to
be around someone who
is (or at least claims
to be) of a different
kind, especially when you
believe that you may
be in love with that someone,
and that if only that someone
were of the same kind, there
could be a melding of souls
that could put time at a standstill.
even if all the signs lead
you to believe one thing, there
must be proof before this one
thing can be labeled fact;
only time can tell, and
who knows—maybe tomorrow
the true self will allow itself to
emerge...

th' bottom line.

twinkle, twinkle little star,
i know you wonder who i are.
i wonder, too, but my brain tends to mar,
as i travel near and far.

days and nights both seem th' same,
their only difference is a name.
when i figure out th' rules of this game,
i'll go back from whence i came.

eyes tell lies that lips can't speak.
a slap is th' same as a kiss on th' cheek.
the english you read just might be greek.
you offer compassion, you're labeled a freak.

th' future is really close at hand.
th' present i still don't understand.
th' past seems like a foreign land.
i assume that all of this was planned…

being fake seems to be all th' rage;
i guess that's why we invented th' stage.
can't tell if i'm inside or outside th' cage—
i guess i'll just have to turn th' page…

the flight of the black dove.

he stands in a crowd of people,
yet he appears to be standing
all by himself.

his beauty transposes all time.

as he walks down the street,
all that is not him is simply
nonexistent,
and the world takes notice.

one foot in front of the other
on the pavement,
yet he floats above the clouds.
clouds of beauty.
clouds of wonder.
clouds of amazingness.

he is confident, sure. certain.
he is love—he is a black dove.
you must love him…

as if carved from
the most exquisite marble,
his skin glows and radiates
a coolness
that verges on perfection.

his walk is more than a walk:
it is a glide which
announces him.

robert l. darden

not a word needs to be spoken.
his presence *is* the conversation,
and even when he's not there,
he is still felt.

he is love.
he is a black dove.
you must love him…

allow me to ramble: part one~love(?)

so. you think you know what love is? you say that you've been loved. you think you're in love right now. this very moment. you've got so much to learn.

love is not half of the joys that you think it is. love is about no longer being an individual. love is about no longer making your own decisions. love is about no longer doing what's right for you.

love is about living for someone else. completely.

"you, singular" has now become "you, plural". 'til death do you part.

that's a long damn time.

they've said "be careful what you wish for" and "more tears are shed over answered prayers":

love is the epitome of what those sayings are about.

you may think that you know what you want; you may think that you want someone to be there each and every moment of each and every day. you may think that you want to get phone calls each hour on the hour, just to be told 'i love you'. you may think that you want to wake up beside, and go to sleep beside, the same person, each morning and evening of the rest of your life.

you may be perfectly right. but, you need to be 100% certain before you make any type of commitment: what you want right now may not be what you're actually looking for. then again, it could be exactly what you're looking for, but are you sure you can handle it? and even if you can handle it, are you *ready* to handle it?

do you know that as easily as people can fall in love, it is just as possible for people to fall out of love? nothing has to change from one point to the other—it just happens.

no rhyme. no reason. just life.

love is not a tangible thing. it's not something that you can physically hold onto, even though you may hold it in your heart and in your mind. you can not actually hold it in your hands: this is what scares the hell out of a lot of the people who attempt to love. the idea that they've given in to something that they can neither hold nor see, yet it takes control over their entire lives.

robert l. darden

    in one way, or several, love is like a religion unto itself; the biggest difference is that love has been around a hell of a lot longer than religion, and love isn't one of man's misguided creations. man's only contribution to love is the on-going complication that gives love its (sometimes) bad reputation.
    these days, people tend to think that they can fix any problem concerning love by just buying some flowers, chocolates, or jewelry, all in the *name* of love. and while these things may make things alright for the moment, the fact of the matter is this: love has all the control, and if you don't know how to love, or most importantly, how to be loved, then you may not be able to keep your love.
    even though you feel that you'll be forever in love…

misjudgment day.

you talk to me as if you knew me,
but you have absolutely no fucking clue:
if you knew half an ounce of what i was
    thinking,
you'd make sure that i never spoke to you.
you say that my smile makes you feel you can
    trust me.
you say that my aura seems perfectly calm.
i say that you're an awful judge of character,
'cause i'd laugh in your face with your heart in
    my palm.
i'm not the sweet baby that you thinks i be;
i'd twice fuck you over to see if twice you'd cry.
if you asked my opinion, i'd be brutally honest,
but your true friends would give you the
    obvious lie…

you categorize my entire existence,
and i'd simply admire your persistence.
your bullshit gets met with no resistance,
and my attitude and apathy will retain their
    consistence.

you look at me as if i were golden,
like there were nothing to you i'd deny.
i could give half a damn 'bout your damn
    situation,
and if you called me for help, you would get
    no reply.
yeah, you see me all smiles, full of laughter and
    charm,

havin' fun with the peoples i do care about,
but you don't fit that profile—i care not about
    you,
so therefore, muh-phucka, yo' ass goes
    widdout...
i'm not sure what it is that makes me dislike you
    so,
and obviously you haven't figured it out.
i'm not about to drop time to work on the
    research,
so just take my word—i do hate you. no doubt.

you can categorize my entire existence,
and i'll simply admire your persistence.
your bullshit will get met with no resistance
as my attitude and apathy retain their
    consistence...

(fuck you)

ascension incognito.

i sit and i wait as the night fills the sky;
just watching the people as they quickly go by.
no notice of me ever enters their eyes,
for i'm sitting there incognito.

hear them talkin' 'bout things they don't think i can hear,
how they're dealin' with demons like mistrust and fear,
tryin' to work through confusions, tryin' to make 'em more clear:
they pretend that it's not about ego.

in the cover of darkness, the lies get more bold,
and the stories more daring each time they're retold.
how much tax did you put on the bullshit you sold?
think how soon you'll be right back @ zero.

by the ease of your flow, still you don't know i'm there,
so you drone on and on like you don't have a care.
you occasionally get loud so that people will stare,
yet you swear you don't want the attention.

so your stories float on like they're caught by the storm,

and you create and polish new aspects of your
    form.
to be free of your spotlight, you'd be out of your
    norm—
you'd just drift to another dimension.

you continue your walk right across your own
    stage;
i approach end of chapter, and, therefore, turn
    the page.
in this book which you've written, you, of
    course, are the rage:
your ego begins its ascension…

progression?

i keep coming back and still i'm not here;
i probably walked right past myself.
i keep looking right at it and still it's not clear,
though it seems to be seen by everyone else…
i wrote all the lyrics and all of the music,
but i can't figure out how to sing the damn song.
i refuse to admit that the fault lies within:
i could not have possibly done something
      wrong…

the dawn of each day seems as dark as its dusk,
though the sun shines brighter each and every
      morn.
each night rolls around putting end to its day,
and although i've done nothing, each day i'm
      more worn.
i look at the pages as the words run together;
i patiently wait 'til they decide to calm down.
i jump into the water and go towards the deep end.
i lay there, just floating; it seems i can't drown…

i open my eyes to look into the silence;
it's a lot more colourful than i thought it would be.
i find myself deciphering all my old mysteries:
as it turns out, i'm not half what i should be.
i walk through the snow in search of the ocean;
i have no idea why i've chosen this path.
i question the voices—i fear that they've left me.
i am not reassured when i hear their cold
      laugh…

i stop to look around and it's all too familiar,
though i've never walked this far out before.
i hear my name being called, but there's no one
    around me,
so now, of my solitude, i'm no longer sure.
my eyes are now closed and i'm no longer
    moving.
my confusion has upgraded itself into fear.
i open my mouth to scream out for help,
and before the last echo, it all disappears…

…i keep coming back and still i'm not here;
i probably walked right past myself…

the cost of global unity.

the olympics—do we really need this oxymoronic display of how to spend too much money on a concepte more tired that those who participate?

for months, the idea of "bringing the world together" is tossed about and played with like so many brightly-coloured beach balls, and once the unity has been bought and the world's finest are assembled, what do they do? *they compete!!* "play *our* anthem!" "raise *our* flag!"—(correctly, if you don't mind…)

colour me shallow, but i just am not able to equate competition with peace and/or global unity. and what exactly does it teach anyone? after all the money has been spent and all the races won, the "victorious" just ride on that *"hello-i'm-fabulous-and-i-have-a-medal!"*-vibe,

and no cures for anything have been discovered!! but, oh!, weren't we entertained?!

(smile for the camera…)

besides, the concepte of giving it up for something more worthwhile after working *so* hard just seems to boggle the mind…

cash in your medals and go buy a clue—

don't forget to check your ego at the border.

the upper hand.

…alone in an elevator, beside you i stand,
and though you don't know me, we talk man-to-man.
as i praise your success, your ego gets fanned;
as you step out, you turn and extend your strong hand…

…these next moments you'll carry for the rest of your days,
and never again will you be more amazed…

at first glance, i may not appear much to you,
so you don't look at me, you just look right through.
if all you take in is the shade of my skin,
you bypass the power that i have within.
to you i don't matter, for you don't know my name,
yet when something goes wrong, it's me that you blame.
but, because you don't know that i, too, play your game,
i now have the upper hand…

you refuse to acknowledge that i live in your town;
if i start to come up, you'll just knock me back down.
in your world, all you see is yourself and not me,
and somehow you believe that's the way it should be.
i may just be someone to whom you'd tell lies,
or someone you'd beat just to see if i'd cry,
but not long from now, you just might realize
that i've got the upper hand….

should've.

you say you want to stay with me
that there's nothin' you won't do for me
you say you'd die if i chose to leave
and you'd buy me the world if you had to

i never came close to feelin' the same
i just came along to play my game
i never even bothered to learn your name
and i regret the fact that i've had you

as easy as it was for you to get to me
i have no idea what you thought we could be
you should've recognized it from the beginning
that this scene was just too weird

you should've known that i would only hurt you
take what i wanted and then desert you
you should've looked and seen who i really
      am—
the one you should've feared...

you wonder where all this is coming from
and i can't believe you could be this dumb
did you not even feel how i just went numb
every time that you tried to touch me?

so now i turn to walk away
disregarding whatever you might have to say
i refuse to turn and look your way
and all you've got is the right to judge me

robert l. darden

as easy as it was for you to get to me
i can not imagine what you thought we'd be
you should've recognized it from the beginning
that this scene was just too weird

you should've known that i would only hurt you
take what i needed and then desert you
should've looked at me for what i really am—
the one you should've feared…

a lover's test…

21 days since last they met ;
he think of him and his eyes become wet.
he turns his sight up to the sky—
he'd always known that he could fly…
he looks at his watch: it's seven-o-three.
he goes and sits beneath a tree,
and as he's there, he begins to feel
that maybe what happened was not real.
things aren't always as they seem ;
perhaps this all was just a dream…

he goes back home to sleep, alone—
he prays for a ring on his telephone :
he hopes that his lover would call and say
that these had been his testing days—
to test his love, by means of depth,
to see if when gone, their love he kept.
but when he arrives, there's no one there :
silently, he climbs the stairs…
the thoughts he's thinking are just so deep
that he goes to bed but can not sleep…
…he awakes, however, just to find
that they'd both been there all this time.
things aren't always what they seem ;
this, in fact, was just a dream…

future in flames.

the world as you know it
shall burst into flames.
we'll tell you our stories—
we might mention names.
striving for equality,
we're ready to fight!
we want the same freedoms :
we demand the same rights!
searching for compassion
with whatever it takes.
always in fashion—
no time for fakes…
in every way possible,
we're taking control, and
nothing will stop us
from reaching our goals.
the world as you know it
shall burst into flames.
we'll tell you our stories—
and we might mention names….

androgyny.

earrings in one ear,
sometimes in two.
big, baggy clothing.
gender-neutral shoes.
hair pulled straight back,
or maybe just there.
a look on the face saying :
"do you think i care?".
matching accessories,
make-up on eyes.
thin, slender bottoms.
thick, muscled thighs.
"is she just butch?"
"is he just a bitch?"
maybe one day they
decided to switch!?
leather and spikes,
ruffles and lace.
my, what a gloriously
androgynous face!
deep, gravely voices,
high, piercing shrills :
ponder th' mystery—
imagine th' thrills…

homogenous.

o.k.; you got your little "froot-loopz", and th'
    rings are in your ears,
and you got a pen to jot some numbers: get up.
    go out, and work it dear!
work it like you had a purpose, work it like you
    did not care,
work it like there's no tomorrow—make those
    bastards stop and stare!
give 'em somethin' to remember. give 'em
    ev'rything you got.
they'll pretend to be embarrassed, but you'll
    know that you got 'em hot!
when it seems th' night is over, find somethin' or
    someone else to do.
ain't no shame in goin' for it, 'cause, baby, it
    belongs to you!
only stop when you get ready—no one tells you
    what to do.
you can shout it from th' rooftops—you're a
    homo diva, "tried" and true!

human unity.

who can determine the difference between right
    and wrong?
why does there have to be one?
today is just the tomorrow of yesterday, thus,
life should be lived to its fullest extent.
no limits. no regrets. no shame.
it should not matter to whom you choose to give
    your love…
what one man deems "imperfect" is another
    man's pure gold—
which of them is wrong?
why does either have to be?
through the eyes of a child, i see my future; a
    future full of…
who knows?
waiting patiently is the only way i'll ever know.
beyond the limits can be peace…

pleasure.

i cling to my need to be in his presence
as if it were my last anticipated breath;
through pleasing him, i myself am pleased…
i love the feeling i get when i make him happy,
even though my eagerness to do so makes him
       uncomfortable.
he is everything i could ever ask for in a lover,
but he's also the big brother i never had—
i do not wish to destroy that.
through pleasing him, i myself am pleased…

the essence of a destiny unknown.

quilts 'n' pillows on th' floor,
nothin' less, yet nothin' more,
except three windows and a door—
can you find what you're lookin' for?
time: she cares not how you feel,
or what you think or believe to be real.
she just keeps rollin' like a wheel,
and never once does she lose her zeal.
now you've decided that you want to play—
th' game is over, so be on your way…
maybe tomorrow, maybe today
you'll find th' words you needed to say.
all this time you've wondered "why?" :
why th' sun shines as clouds roll by?
why people live until they die?
why fish swim? and why birds fly?
when you find the answers, let me know,
then we can get together and go
to search for th' wind (if it decides to blow)—
it ain't gonna be easy though…

karma.

pressed against a total stranger,
dancin' in a spinnin' room.
unaware of present danger,
unmindful of impending doom.

your mind's full of thoughts you can't control—
try as you may, you can not flee.
your dancin' partner is your soul,
and he is havin' his way with thee…

you try to stop but you can't fight it;
dealin' with forces much stronger than you.
subconsciously, you are delighted,
doin' things you never dared to do…

to and fro across the floor—
the music moves you here and there:
as you go beyond the door,
you realize you haven't a prayer…

seasons of sorrow (I-IV).

I. l'ete.

...walking along a sun-drenched beach, a young man trips (on a seashell) and falls to the ground. each grain of sand that he wipes from his eyes reminds him of each of the men who pushed him aside for the love of another. he picks himself up, and continues along the beach...

II. l'automne.

...seeing the leaves falling from the trees, a young man recalls the numerous occasions that he has had his heart broken and blown away, and he begins to (silently) weep. as the leaves scrape away his tears, he walks on...

III. l'hiver.

...upon strolling through the forest on a cold and frosty winter morning, a young man hears reminders of his past relationships—symbolized by the sounds of his feet on the frozen twigs and icy snow beneath: he walks on...

IV. les printemps.

...as the snow begins to melt away to reveal the earth, a young man is reminded of the countless hours spent crying over men who have broken his heart. while the birds sing, he begins to walk away...

the value of friendship.

that tree
in the woods
is home to a bird;
that bird
does not mind
sharing his home with others
(as long as the others
are respectful of
his house…).

censorship: a realist's p.o.v.

a work of art is the equivalent of a dream,
and, therefore, can not be censored;
you can not control a dream,
but you can wake th' fuck up!!!

cogitations.

stood in the rain for so damn long
that once again i became dry;
still can't determine whether it's rain
or a tear that's in my eye…

picked up a stone and tossed it away,
just to see how far it would go:
could not tell if it landed or not,
and today i still don't know…

still trying to determine the purpose of sex—
is it punishment or is it reward?
it feels too good to be all bad,
but why the hell is it so damned hard??

disillusional dismay.

at times i wonder
who knows (really)
who i am.
at times i wonder
if *i* know (really)
who i am.
there's a strong fear
of finding
that things are not
what they seem.
there, too, is a strong fear
of realizing that i am
fearing what would happen
if those who know me
really got to know me:
then i realize that
i really don't give a damn!

wishful thinking.

one day, when the time is right, one voice will be the only voice that can be heard. it will be a voice of many colours and it will know no boundaries, for it shall belong to all. it will know no shame, for it shall be pure in each and every way. but until that one day, we must each use the one voice which we each have, and hope that when our turn comes about, whatever we find the courage to say will make a difference…

wishful thinking: part 2.

from the darkness is heard a cry. it's not a cry of sorrow, pain, or fear, nor is it a cry of regret. it is a cry of freedom which signifies that the world is waking up from the deep, deep coma that she's been in for too damn long. her cry calls for change and demands justice. it promises to educate as it yearns for consistency. her heartbeat can be felt all over: ignorance and despair shall be no more…

III~ii~I (three-to-one).

…as III, they stood tall. fearless and proud. they had been through heaven as III; likewise, as III, they had been through hell. but the entire time, they were together: III. weathering fierce and unnecessary criticisms because they were 'different'. and in the end, when I of the III was called away, he feared nothing—he only asked that the remaining ii not cry—4 someday, they would again be III…

things have always been this way...

rainbows shattered
on th' ground.
pain and sorrow
all around.
darkness throughout
the entire day:
things have always been this way...

children dying,
no reason at all.
planes in mid-air
just start to fall.
it does not matter
what we say:
things have always been this way...

poverty. famine.
they rule th' lands.
people ignoring
the outstretched hands.
seems just like
any other day:
things have always been this way...

suddenly someone speaks his mind.
cures for diseases we begin to find.
now all the children, together they play;
things will never be the same...

dining on unity.

a cup. a saucer. a plate. a bowl.
each individual, yet part of a whole.
each has its own purpose, each has its own size,
yet all four can be used at the very same time.
once, covered with food and filled up with drink,
they again come together within the dish-sink...

the frantic cycle./the fear of being fearless.

i know that freedom doesn't come for free,
but i refuse to be forced to pay to be me :
i know who i am.
i'm not afraid of this man,
'cause it's through his eyes that i see…

to be happy these days takes a whole lot of
        planning,
and there's quite a few people who just are not
        understanding
that my life's about me.
they just will not agree
when it's not their egos that i'm fanning…

some people are beginning to realize,
and the others are going to be mighty surprised :
it's not wrong to think clearly,
or to live one's life queerly,
and i have no need for alibis…

i'm afraid that i just might be fearless.
my absence of smile doesn't render me cheerless.
i'll beat you at your game,
achieve my own type of fame,
and when it's over, my eyes shall be tearless…

overcome...

insecurity just fucked arrogance right up the ass,
just walked right up to him and said "hey, let's
    dance."
took him by his fat hand, then took control of
    his pants.
did him right then and there. had the nerve.
    took the chance.
contentment just bitch-slapped mistrust and
    deceit,
just walked right up to them, knock'd 'em both
    off their feet.
shouted obscenities. carried on, down the street.
soundtrack playing in head: *victory, bittersweet.*

desire sits dateless. lust goes unfulfilled.
jealousy has a fever. greed endures overkill.
pain just went on vacation. hunger just came
    from lunch.
fatigue was running toward salvation; horny
    beat it to the punch.
sobriety planned a great party, but of course, no
    one came.
concern bleeds in the corner: apathy just won
    the game....

would you...?

would you recognize love if he walked through your door,
took all of his clothes, threw them down on the floor?
if he said all the things you've been dying to hear,
would you walk over to him, or sit blinded by fear?
is it possible that love could be with you right now,
and you'd give him love back, if you only knew how?
would you know how to answer if love called your name,
or would you even hear him over the noise of your games?
would you honestly say you've experienced true love?
that there was or is someone you thought the world of?
if that person came to you to see you today,
would you have any idea of what you should say?
could you look into his eyes and see past your reflection?
would you admit you were wrong if he raised an objection?
would you knock down your walls if you knew they'd reveal him?
could you stand side-by-side and not touch him, yet feel him?

would you dance to the songs his heart sings to
    yours?
would you give him the keys to unlock all your
    doors?
could you look at his flaws and not ask him to
    lose them?
would you dismiss his choices if you don't also
    choose them?
could you stand where he's standing and still be
    who you are?
would you dare share the stage, or should you be
    the star?
could you give in to feelings you don't usually
    show?
would you even admit them, heaven forbid you
    should grow?
would you recognize love if he walked through
    your door,
or would you just sit there, waiting, as if you
    deserved more?

my man and his way...

the way that he looks when he calls out my
    name.
the way that he tastes after i do the same.
the way that i love him leaves no room for the
    games.
i love him that much. i leaves nothin' to shame.

the way that he feels when my dick's in his ass.
the hunger i have when his dick's in my grasp.
the way that he enters me, making me gasp.
the power he wields when our hands are clasped.

the way that he shivers when my tongue meets
    his thigh.
the way my heart quivers when me meet eye-to-
    eye.
the way that he cums and just lets that shit fly.
the way he's my drug. and i yearn to be high.

reflections, in the key of me minor: part 1.

i look in the mirror, but all that i see
is the face of some guy who looks a whole lot
    like me,
therefore, he's familiar—just how, i can't 'splain,
so i stand and i stare, but he does just the same.

"turn away. walk away. go away. leave me be"
is all i can say to this guy lookin' like me.
no response is his answer. no emotion, his mask.
then i'm flooded with questions that i dare not
    to ask.

so we both stand defiant, refusing to give.
both claiming possession of this life, most ill-
    lived.
i turn and walk away from this guy and his stare;
though i no longer see him, i can feel he's still
    there.

so i run out the door, hoping he doesn't follow:
i can still feel his presence. i begin to feel
    hollow…
i look around for his shadow, but i only see
    mine.
i'm still running and running, running right out
    of time.

i decide to stop running, take a break, catch my
    breath.
when i do, i realize that there's no daylight left.
i feel i should go home, where i hope i'll be safe,

cursed blessings/blessed curses

then i wonder: "what if we two share more than
    a face?"

how can i get away from all he is (or has been)?
every time that i see him, he's wrapped in my
    skin…

…i go back to the glass, and sure enough, he's
    still there,
and with eyes like my own, he affixes his stare.
i know i can't run away, i know i can not hide:
everything that is him is everything that is i…

…i want to talk to him, parlay, see what all this
    is about;
when i do try to speak, he stands there open-
    mouthed.
suddenly, we're both screaming and shouting
    and cursing.
his every move mimics mine—i think he's been
    rehearsing…

to no avail, i attempt conversation again,
yet i speak not a word. for the moment, he
    wins…

(to be continued…)

to be legendary.

to be loved you must love, yet to live you must
    die.
if you know what is true, then you, too, know
    the lie.
to be your own legend, you must step away from
    self,
and endure your comparisons 'gainst everyone
    else.

…at this moment, i am just not sure
how much more of this shit to endure.
sifting through motives not entirely pure,
i find, all at once, disease and it's cure…

how long?...

how long should i wait before i tell him i love him?
how long should it be before those words hit the air?
how long can i silently lay here beside him,
when i already know that he knows that i care...(?)

indulgencia.

as their hands clasp together, there is that
    familiar shortness of breath which can
    only be interpreted as sublime union.
their bodies move together and separate (freely.
    frantically.) to create a pain that is every
    bit as deliciously intense as it is mind-
    wrenching. dripping wet with emotion,
    they scream "i love you" and other things
    much less cohesive, but very much
    understood: it's the most intimate level of
    oneness—till death do them part…

outside.

staring out a window,
seeing all of nature,
watching the animals,
and the birds, and
their interactions—
wishing. hoping. praying
that you could find
someone to share all
of this with. even
the trees seem to be
in on the game/joke;
swaying to and fro
on the complexingly
aromatic breeze.
and the birds, flying
overhead in the sky
cause you to contemplate
soaring through and
above the clouds—
and then you plummet back
down to reality; you close
the curtains and go back
to bed—alone. again.
(and then, you cry…)

masquerade.

every time that you've seen me i was wearing a
    smile,
i seemed as happy as happy can be.
but this body of man with its soul of a child
was just hiding its true misery.

i would laugh and be silly, the center of
    attention,
that's usually where you could find me,
and that mask of the fool wouldn't allow me to
    mention
that my pain and my tears almost blind me.

i would offer a shoulder if you needed to cry—
all your problems i would try to solve.
but i'd run from *my* problems, i'd rather just die.
fade to black. turn to dust: dissolve…

forbidden tongue.

the answer to a question that i ask over and over
    is printed, in plain sight, in front of my face,
    in a language which i know not how to speak;
as i teach myself this particular tongue, the words
    begin to fade away—almost as if to say that
    i'm better off not knowing the answer…

to have and have not.

…if a thought remains stagnant, unspoken too
 long,
its value and strength just grow less and less
 strong.
in a while, even to you, it begins to seem wrong,
and you doubt all the things you've been
 knowing…

i compromise everything so that you can be
 happy,
and as a result, i never am.
i cry every night, with no tears, as i slumber—
all as the result of my giving a damn.
i've prayed countless times that it all would be
 over;
i've tried to impede this through my own hand.
yet every time, my hand lacks the courage
to carry through what my mind had in plan.

i may not be black in your conventional sense,
but i *am* black—past, present, and future tense.
you cast me aside 'cause you don't understand
that my differences don't make me any less of a
 man.
my views and beliefs don't sit easy with you;
my ideals and visions may frighten you, too:
to be all that i am in a world you designed
keeps you searching for answers that you just
 may not find,

so, i'm going to say what i damn well please.

cursed blessings/blessed curses

no apologies to you if i cause you 'unease',
but through these two eyes, i'm the one who sees
where i am and where i'm going…

when you're walking ahead, but still looking
    back,
you'll eventually, inevitably, walk right off your
    track.
when you open your eyes, all you'll see is pure
    black,
though for days upon days it's been snowing…

2001:begin anew.

...in the 8th month of the year the millennium
    actually begins,
i will officially have lived 3 decades in this same
    skin;
for all that that's worth, what do i have to show?
everything that i have could leave when the wind
    blows...

today is the perfect day to begin anew:
what choice do you really have?
you can not go back, you can only go forward,
so why not create a brand new path?

for all the troubles in your past,
you've really only your self to blame;
even though there were others you thought were
    at fault,
it was you chose to succumb to their games.

wipe your slate clean and make a fresh start.
hold no one accountable except for yourself.
that way if you fail, you can kick your own ass;
but when you win, you won't have to thank
    anyone else...

wrong from the start.

your love is supposed to validate my existence?
is that why i brought you through my door?
you say you admired my persistence,
but is that all you were looking for?

the words you speak seem too rehearsed—
exactly what you thought i would want to hear,
but with all the emotion you've dispersed,
i have no option but to fear…

what did you think when you saw me there?
that because we both wanted it, i'd have to care?
what made you think that i'd treat you fair?
you thought your money could buy my heart?

what was it you thought you stood to gain?
to go along, as i did, i must be insane.
and although you blame me for all of your pain,
you should have known it was wrong from the
        start…

lovelust.

love ain't tryin' t'pay my bills.
love ain't off'rin no new thrills.
love ain't takin' me over no hills,
so love just ain't gon' do…

lust is keepin' me up on my toes.
lust is reteachin' what i already know.
lust is takin' me high from my low—
yeah, lust is gettin' me through…

love ain't th'reason i get outta bed.
love ain't th'butter that melts on my bread.
love ain't th'music that plays in my head,
so love need not call my name…

lust is th'reason i'm out in th'streets;
lust is th'reason i sometimes don't eat;
lust is th'reason you're stuck t'my sheets:
yes, lust be th'name of my game.

love used t'be here, but love went away.
love may come back, but who knows if he'll
      stay…
love *is* a part of me, but no, not today:
love's bein' push'd t'th'side.

lust is th'voice which keeps callin' my name.
lust is th'force walkin' me thru th'rain.
lust straddles th'bound'ry of pleasure n' pain—
and my lust just will not be denied…

the power/your eyes.

your eyes have the power to make me feel
    strong,
even while i am feeling that i just don't belong.
when it seems that all that i do is done wrong,
your eyes give me all that i need to go on.

your eyes have the power to brighten my day,
even when it appears nothing's going my way.
encouraging in a manner that the mouth needs
    not say,
your eyes lift me up with their beautiful display.

your eyes have the power to make my heart
    dance,
even while i'm assuming my most difficult
    stance.
as i wonder on whether to make an advance,
your eyes give me the confidence to take that
    chance.

your eyes have the power to comfort my soul,
even when i feel that i've lost all control.
when my spirit is shattered and i start to unfold,
your eyes have the power to make me feel whole.

how?

which of our senses has control
when we're in the dark?
blindness enhances our other senses,
but so much of what we do
is instinct that all is lost
in the moment…

how can we know what we
should or should not
reach for in the dark?
if we touch that which
causes us pain,
what's the point of screaming—
how do we know if we'll be heard?

is it that we simply can not see,
or that our eyes
(and our minds)
remain closed?
how can you know in pitch darkness
if you've blinked?

how can i fathom where i'm going,
having no grasp of where i've been?
how can i believe all the things i've been
      knowing,
when i have no idea how i got into this skin?

the hunger.

a hunger
so powerful
that nothing else exists.
blood as thick as chocolate
runs through veins
at a speed which
causes one to
throw all morality
aside, and do
what they deem
necessary to keep
the craving under control…

a hunger
so intense
that all else is irrelevant.
no boundaries or limits
to be spoken of:
dream and fantasy
become reality
in a world where
happiness can be as
hard to obtain as
the right shade of paint…

a hunger
so mighty
that nothing else matters.
emotional chaos alongside
rationalizations considered ill-advised
by those not

robert l. darden

in search of the feaste…

…a feaste so bountiful
that millions could be fed;
but the hunger is so great
that one's desire is never
completely satiated…

apology not offered.

i refuse to apologize
for seeing my life through my own two eyes.
my dreams are dreamt in my own head,
during sleep that is slept in my own bed.
i walk through my life on my own two feet.
my heart beats only to its own beat.

an observation…

sitting. remaining the silent
one in a conversation
about nothing, which is
being held, coincidentally,
by those who claim to
know everything:
such is life….

innocence.

music flows through the air
like a breeze on which
the opaque aroma of
melancholy delight and
haphazard conceit are
fused together…

by the time the end
is averted,
the dance has begun…

soliloquy.

poor, lonely, innocent soul;
tried so hard, a heart of gold…
confused, misused, kept in the dark:
eyes once sparkled, now, no spark…
tears of sorrow in those eyes.
asked many questions—was told many lies…
reached out to one considered a friend;
found out how far the truth can bend…

kept on trying all the while:
even through the pain, she smiled…

untitled…

there are things that you don't know that i do
    know—
but you don't know that i know;
there are things that you and i both know—
but i pretend not to know;
there are things that you know, or at least think
    you know,
but you'll never know for sure;
there are things that you know that i need to
    know—
but i just don't care anymore…

there are times when i love you with all of my
    heart;
there are times when your name causes hatred to
    start.
there are times that there's not much for you i
    wouldn't do;
there are times that i can't stand the mere
    thought of you.

there's a point in one's life when he must be set
    free,
to see how far he can go believing what he
    believes.
then, if he can add to things he has known,
he can say that his life is truly his own.

blackness looking back at me...

crawling through a sea of mud,
ice cubes stop the flow of blood.
teardrops frozen on my face.
no light at all inside this space.
voices hail from every side,
yet none as loud as those inside.
rocks beneath my hands and knees.
my breathless words in mid-air freeze.
i open my eyes and all i see
is blackness looking back at me...

standing alongside childhood friends,
reminiscing on days that had no ends.
wrinkles of happiness cover my face.
sunshine abounds from ground to space.
laughter bounces off every hill,
and no mere words can contain the thrill.
wading through rippling reflections of trees,
i'm stopped by an almost melodic breeze:
down into the water, i look and i see
my reflection, in blackness, looking back at
    me...

tired.

tired of being a token.
i want to be who i am;
i want to be what i am:
me!

tired of being patronized.
i want the things which
are said to me to be sincere,
not just said to make me feel better:
do not lie to me!!

tired of pretending to be someone i'm not.
this is me—see me. love me!!!

someday, it will all end…(?)

an annoyance.

water from a
dripping faucet
will, eventually,
fill an empty glass.
but the amount of
time that it takes
can be just as
annoying as the slow
'plop-plop-plop'
that can be heard
throughout the
silent, empty house…

an annoyance: updated/rethought.

water from a leaky faucet
will eventually fill an empty glass,
but the sound that it makes
and the time that it takes
are simply fucking annoying!

allow me you…

allow me to cause you to feel emotions you
     never knew that you
  possessed.
allow me to give you new names for old feelings
     you never had the
  means to express.
allow me to touch you. allow me to hold you.
      allow yourself to be
  caressed;
allow me you…

allow me to kiss away sleep in the morning,
      while a new day begins
  and the night is now past.
allow me to be there as new nights are falling,
     reassuring that
  happiness is within your grasp.
allow me to serve you. allow me to please you.
      allow yourself never
  the need to ask;
allow me you…

allow me the taste of your salty-sweet skin, as
     sweat trickles down
  to the small of your back.
allow me the sight of your body by moonlight as
     the clouds
  disappear and the eve fades to black.
allow me to sense you. allow me to send you.
      allow yourself to let
  me bring you back;

cursed blessings/blessed curses

allow me you…

allow yourself fresh air to breath.
allow yourself new worlds to conceive.
allow yourself fantasies to be believed.
allow yourself my love to receive.

allow me to dance in and out of your brain.
allow me to cause you no cause to complain.
allow me to walk with you, sunshine and rain.
allow me your pleasures. allow me your pains.
allow yourself all of your own bells to ring.
allow me to you new music to bring.
allow yourself a brand new song to sing.
allow me to give you my everything:

allow me you…

a message to my people....

sister, my sister. my beautiful sister.
depend on yourself, don't sit waiting for mister.
everything that you want, everything you could
    need,
already belongs to you—just don't give in to
    greed.
let your mind be you ticket; let your heart be
    your guide.
let your eyes be wide open and you won't be
    denied...

brother, my brother. my powerful brother.
stand up and be yourself, don't be played by
    another.
it really doesn't matter how much 'ice' you got—
what's going to happen when it starts to get hot?
true status is judged by what you have in your
    head:
that's the one thing they can't take when from
    this world you're led...

you won't recognize me, but i recognize you.
i don't speak like you speak, but i do speak the
    truth,
and i speak to you now as a man independent,
but this does not make me black man non-
    descendant.
i come from the same people and places you
    do—
all that is inside of you resides in me, too.

cursed blessings/blessed curses

give up the all the attitude. stop playing the
>games.
look me right in the eyes and learn more than
>my name.
but if you don't know yourself, how can you
>know another?
you are stuck where you are because of you and
>no other.
don't hate me for creating a path of my own—
all that time spent on hate just might leave you
>alone…

don't talk about unity unless you know how it's
>done:
if you're no good for you, then you're good for
>no one.
for me to help you, i've got to know who i am,
and for you to help yourself, you've got to give a
>damn.
you're only going to go as far as you allow;
it all depends on you—i can not tell you how…

the past may have answers to questions of old,
and the past may hold keys that can unlock the
>soul,
but my past is a bridge which burns as we
>speak—
i can only go forward for the knowledge i seek.
we all need to let go of the shit that was 'then'
and reach deep for the strength to let our lives
>begin.

homo sects, you all.

to look at him, there's no way you could know,
but then again, you just may.
he did his job just as well as you did,
but he lost that job just because he is gay.

she sets her goals high. she goes far beyond
     them.
each day she does all that she can.
she acknowledges your god. she serves her
     country.
never once has she ever wished she were a man.

he pays his bills. he pays his taxes.
he pays for all of his own meals.
but all that seems to matter is who he fucks,
to hell with what he thinks or feels.

she drives a truck. she swings a hammer.
she does the shit she needs to do.
she washes her face and puts on some make-up,
but still she's not good enough for you.

he paints his face. he paints his toenails,
then "she" paints the town as red as hell.
"she" goes back home, turns back into him,
bursting with stories he could never tell…

she sings her songs of "him" and "his",
though "her" and "hers" is what she feels:
her mouth may say what's written for her,

cursed blessings/blessed curses

but in her eyes the truth gets revealed…

he rides the bus to school every morning
and lies about the girl he had last night,
but the last dream he had starred the boy now
    beside him,
and although they tangled, it wasn't a fight.

she bakes her own pastries. she made her own
    curtains.
she sewed her own seat covers for her new car.
she sips her beer slowly—she bought it herself.
she winks at your girl as she puffs her cigar…

he built your computer. he worked on your
    plumbing.
he said what was wrong with, and then fixed,
    your car.
he built his own house. he hunts his own food.
yet he still isn't man enough to fight in your
    wars…

they go to church, and they read the scripture;
they know the bible's every word.
they cry out for help. they cry out for freedom.
their voices are seldom, if ever, heard.

we have the same dreams. we have the same
    feelings.
we just, sometimes, express them in different
    ways.
we are not the enemy. we are fellow humans—
we just happen to be lesbian and gay…

shadows.

preconceived is your image of me,
therefore you refuse to love me.
don't really know anything of me:
place yourself on a pedestal, high above me.
you shield your children, won't let me near them,
even though the right way i could steer them.
call me names—thinking i can't hear them.
play your games—thinking i should fear them.

think you're so much better than me.
won't even try to understand me.
always quick to reprimand me.
from your house and life you've banned me.
the past seems like a foreign land;
the present is just too hard to understand;
the future is really close at hand:
what we need to do is change our plans…

i am not a shadow.
i'm a man. there's blood running through my veins.
believe it or not, i'm very much like you.
i've got visions and dreams.
i've got fears and pains.

tired of living in the shadows.
i deserve to be seen,
standing beside you in the light.
knock down the walls.
open the doors and come on through.
if we all just work together,
then maybe we all could survive.

face of the enemy.

who do you see when you look in the mirror?
could the face of the enemy be seen any clearer?
could the cause of your problems stand right
    where you stand?
do you owe all your heartache and pain to this
    man?
is this person responsible for shattering your
    dreams
the same man who offers his voice for your
    screams?
you sit and you wonder why the world's turned
    against you:
the truth of the matter is that the enemy's within
    you.
he knows how you think, knows your every
    move.
he can sense all your actions, he fits right into
    your groove.

you feel you get cheated because of how you
    look,
but you just can not see you're being read like a
    book.
the cause of your problems hits much closer
    than home,
for the blame and the fault can be claimed as
    your own.

whose voice do you hear when the enemy taunts
    you?

the voice of that face in the mirror which haunts
    you?
how can you convince him to leave you alone
when all that you loathe about him is your very
    own?
you spend far too much effort on placing the
    blame
when it all can reside right beside your sweet
    name.
you're pointing the finger at everyone else,
but you'd see who's at fault if you looked at
    yourself.
how to begin to get rid of your foe
is a question whose answer you should already
    know:

until you change your outlook and begin to love
    yourself,
you are not going to get love from anywhere
    else.
these problems will end if you just let him go,
and you'll experience the greatest love that you'll
    ever know…

ease my pain.

you said that you could stop my tears
and chase away each and all of my fears.
you said that you could heal my pain,
that never would i cry again.
you tried your best to make me smile,
you even cut through my denial.

my troubles, supposedly, a thing of the past,
so never again would i need my mask.
the comfort you offered and said you could give
was an end to the only life i knew how to live.
the pain which you wanted so badly to end
was my most dependable and consistent friend.

to know love...

to know love
to know how love feels
to know the pain it causes
(to know) the beauty it reveals

the need...

i feel a strong need to step
away from reality:
reality is certainly
no friend of mine.
poisoned ice-water crawls
through my veins,
yet i'm expected to smile
as though all is fine.

i'm so tired of always
being good at whatever,
yet always feeling
just like i have failed.
i try and i try
to build a real future,
but it's through my own flesh
that i'm pounding the nails...

misled you.

you stand on that stage as your audience ignores
    you,
and you go on and on 'bout how they adore you.
you talk of your ventures and how you are
    cherished,
but you seem to've forgotten that you should be
    embarrassed…

when me met. [for my husband]

shortly after we met,
we discovered that we
share a brain;
shortly after that,
we began to
share a heart;
from now throughout eternity,
we will
share a life;
i love you so much…

from nothing to something…

…when you found me, i was nothing;
you took me in.
i thought it was because
you knew me.
i know now that you
felt sorry for me:
i do not need your pity…

…when you found me, i had nothing;
you provided for me.
i thought it was because
you liked me.
i know now that you
felt obligated:
i do not need your charity…

…when you found me, i knew nothing;
you tried to teach me.
i thought that this
was genuine.
i know now that
it wasn't:
i do not need your ambiguity…

…as i leave you, i take nothing;
i'm back to where
i started.
all you gave me,
i return to you.
it's time i live my own life:
i do not need your permission…

cursed blessings/blessed curses

…if again you find me, i'll have something;
something that you couldn't give me.
i'll know who i am.
i'll know what i'm doing:
i won't need your approval.

beautiful beaste.

enemy. friend. one and the same.
the beautiful beaste who knows more than your
    name.
his habits, so wild, they dare not be tamed,
that you go along willingly, playing his game.
the smile he possesses leads you to believe
that he wants not to give, yet expects to receive.
once this night is over, though you'll feel you
    should grieve,
your heart allows only that you be relieved.
places you've never dreamed of before
seem as close and familiar as your grocery store.
the people who point at you, calling you
    "whore",
are the same ones who will later come knock on
    your door.
obsession flows freely from woman and man;
aggression takes hold of your hot, sweaty hands;
confessions, so bold, you remain in demand,
'til depression delivers you back where you
    began…
enemy. friend. clearly, now, not the same.
the beautiful beaste has forgotten your name.
the pride you once felt gets replaced by your
    shame,
as you sit all alone, with your damn self to
    blame…

acknowledgment.

acknowledge that you are not the one
   who causes the rising of the sun.
acknowledge that there is no real shame
   in finding that you can't win this game.
acknowledge that you need to fear
   the things which you can't see or hear.
acknowledge that now is your time
   to find your light and let it shine.

acknowledge all you have within.
acknowledge the life outside your skin.
acknowledge the things you see each day.
acknowledge that there may be an easier way.
acknowledge that beginnings are the results of
   ends.
acknowledge your enemies and treat them like
   friends.
acknowledge that there are things which you
   don't know.
acknowledge that comfort is your friend and
   your foe.
acknowledge that positivity isn't always a plus.
acknowledge the constant need to make a big
   fuss.
acknowledge that your future is in your control.
acknowledge that your destiny depends on your
   soul.
acknowledge me. acknowledge yourself.
acknowledge that you don't need anyone else.
acknowledge your power. acknowledge your
   voice.

acknowledge that you do have more than one
    choice.
acknowledge temptation. acknowledge desire.
acknowledge that flame can't exist without fire.
acknowledge that pain is your most consistent
    friend.
acknowledge that one day all the pain will just
    end…

the other side...

the sound that you hear when no noise is made.
the freedom you feel when you're locked in your cage.
the light which shines on you when the moon blocks the sun.
the speed at which you travel when no longer you run.
the taste of an orange when an apple you bite.
the naivete of day. the wisdom of night.
the lyric and vocal performed by the strings.
the melody and harmony that the soloist sings.
the images seen while alone in the dark.
the fire ignited in the absence of spark.
the raindrops which fall while the sun guards the sky.
the vision seen clearly, but not through your eye.
the water you drink when your thirst has been tamed.
the victory of forfeiting your favorite game.
the flavors of foods that you're allowed not to eat.
the importance of shoes to a man with no feet.

the face in the crowd that looks like all the rest.
the answers to questions which are not on the test.
the breeze that surrounds you when the wind doesn't blow.
the desire to be perform and yet not be the show.
the clarity that's there when you roll out of bed.
the recordings of words which have never been said.
the novelty of things which you've done all your life.
the depth of a cut from a dull butter-knife.
the pause button you push in the middle of a dream.
the comfort of not being able to scream.
the connection you feel amongst folks you don't know.
the angst of fast forward when it plays too damn slow.
the warmth of an ice-cube, just beginning to melt.
the horror of feelings you didn't know you felt.

the bitter taste of oxygen when you can't catch your breath.
the calmness of knowing you're seconds from death.
the trust you give people 'though you know it's all lies.
the harshness of sunlight when you first open your eyes.
the darkness of sunrise when you live in a cave.
the coldness of the moonlight when you're fresh in your grave.
the passion and heat of a love that's gone stale.
the confusion of a dog that just can't catch his own tail.
the power of having absolutely no choice.
the message you'd send if you could just find your voice.
the laws which get broken in the name of good fun.
the fat lady singing, 'though it all just begun....

shades...

ebony.
cinnamon.
paper-sack brown.
coffee.
coal.
beige.
schwarz.
bronze.
chocolate.
nutmeg.
midnight.
camel.
negra.
golden.
black.
tar.
latte.
brown.
cola.
cork-board.
eggplant.
mocha.
tan.
black-on-black.
mahogany.
buttercreme.
jet.
copper.
stone.
charcoal.
noire.

robert l. darden

sand.
cafe au lait.
blue-black.
amber.
shadow-black.
khaki.
caramel.
onyx.
creme de cacao.
ashy black.
mocha latte.
cream.
butterscotch.
beyond black…

…different faces and names.
different shade of the same.
different backgrounds and futures.
all with one common claim…

all and nothing…

all is not right
and yet nothing is wrong,
but the words disagree
with the tune of the song.

the trees turn their backs
on a sun that won't shine,
so the clouds float away,
for no warmth do they find.

the waters stand still
and the birds do not sing:
when you walked away,
you took everything…

m.perfection.

...i do not seek out perfect form,
for perfect form i do not possess;
if perfect form is your top priority,
you are not the object of my obsess...

twenty-four double-negative.

the sun comes up and attempts to make dry
any tears that may fall from my unsmiling eyes.
too many forces with which not to comply,
so i look up and thank her for stopping by.

for a very brief moment, there's joy in my heart,
and i question why it was not there from the start.
why have i lived for so long in the dark?
was this penalty for playing all the wrong parts?

i guess with my mirth i should have been content,
but too late for that now, 'cause away it just went.
i'll never know exactly what it was that you meant
by the things that you said when my back was bent…

things can all change in the span of a verse—
just karma's way to reimburse?
perhaps it was all just part of the curse:
for things to get better, they have to get worse.

though i now know happiness as well as sorrow,
i have no idea which will be mine tomorrow.
if you need a teardrop, i've a few you could borrow
as you walk your new path and suggest i don't
      follow…

…lonely doesn't begin to describe the way i feel since
      gone you've been.
you took me to heaven, then just walked away, and
      now there's nothing left within.

robert l. darden

desires i feel, too strong to ignore, each time your voice
    finds its way to my ear.
your presence, so real, all around me, each moment: i
    search, just to find i'm the only one here.

songs without music. windows with no views. i look
    through the mirror—the image i see?
a face with no features; a son that can't shine. a beach
    with no sand. a forest without trees.

…appearing to be on her long journey down,
the sun dries the puddles which sit on the ground:
the rain was my friend, concealing my tears—
too bad it didn't rain all twenty-four years…

twenty-four years of a life gone by.
twenty-four years of tears and sighs.
twenty-four years spent wondering why.
twenty-four years: many lows, too few highs…

somewhere between the front and the back—
no desire to lead, but won't follow the pack.
lost in the crowd, but no denying the fact:
"he seems nice enough, but he's queer and he's black!"

eyes full of tears refusing to flow.
eyes full of fears that the lips won't let go.
eyes full of pain that the heart just won't show—
were it not for the pen, would anyone know?

on the real.

you have to make a choice,
but which one will you make?
will you finally get real,
or go on being fake?
will the lies just go on
'til you believe 'em yourself?
will you ever realize
you're only hurting yourself?
does it matter where you wake
or only that you sleep?
does it matter that
nothing you buy can you keep?
do you feel any better
just because 'they' were near?
do you know that the real
conversations you don't hear?
when all eyes fell upon you,
did you fill up with mirth?
did the fact that 'they' noticed you
add to your worth?
can you honestly match
any name to one face
of those people who so painfully
allow you their space?
do you not know the names
you get called when not there?
well, you're part of that crowd,
so i guess you don't care…

are you happy just being
the friend of the hour?

robert l. darden

do you think you can break through
to some new social power?
do your pockets, once 'phat,'
now seem worse for the wear?
have you anything to show?
do you think that 'they' care?
does you common sense get beat down
by ego and greed?
your mind; 'their' opinions:
which should you now feed?
the more you try to impress them,
the less likely they'll get it,
so just be your true self
and you'll never regret it…

fast forward.

i invited you in. we performed a few sins.
you got tense when i said you could leave.
didn't want you to stay; it did not swing that way,
so your coat and your keys i retrieved.
as you walked 'cross the floor, on your way to the door,
you turned and you asked "what's the deal?";
i said "the deal has been done, and while i did have much fun,
no emotions for you do i feel."
you reply "that's unfair" which brings my "i don't care,
'cause you've known me for less than a week.
this was not about love—what were *you* thinking of?",
and i laugh as you call me a freak.
you get mad and you huff, and then throw down your stuff,
demanding that i apologize.
i say "you must be dense! there was no false pretense."
in this round, you do not win the prize…

with your stuff i once more make your way to my door,
an attempt to show you the way out.
as you stand there, i wonder: is it a spell that you're under?
could it be that my love is that stout?
then you ask "can't we talk?", and i say "yeah, as you walk."
you explain how you think 'we' could 'work'.
i say "i don't think so. for the last time, please go!"
as you walk by, you call me a jerk.
as i am not deterred, you *won't* have the last word.
i look right in your eyes and i say:
"no, we can not be friends, and as this message ends,
please fast forward to the end of our date…"

negative~positivity.

…though my face will be global,
you will not know my name.
i shall taste all your victory,
but i won't play your game.
when my words reach your ears,
you will not hear a sound.
from the bottom of your ocean,
hear me say i won't drown.
as i walk right beside you,
you will not know i'm there.
you will feel when i push you,
but you won't know from where.
while you think what you're thinking,
i'm performing your thoughts.
you'll be aware of my presence,
but of my face you'll know naught…

…i'll reach into your aura
and i'll tickle your soul.
though you make your decisions,
i have all the control.
things around you will move
but you won't know by whose hand,
and you'll find you can't finish
all the things you began.
when you finally see me,
you will not understand:
you'll look right into my eyes,
though behind you i'll stand.
i shall taste all your victory,
but i will not play your game,
and though my face will be global,
you will not know my name…

as forever unbalanced...

almost as if she knew
what was about to happen,
the sun was rapidly sinking,
changing what had been
a beautifully normal day
into what would be remembered as
an unpleasant evening.

the kitchen table had been cleared;
all the dishes were washed and put away...

the entire family was out
on the front lawn.
the children were running
and yelling, as children
are oft allowed to do...

everyone saw the car coming
down the street—
it was a car that was well-recognized,
and respected was the owner—
yet, no one could have known of the
impending failure of the brakes,
which decided to occur
just as one of the children
went running to retrieve
a ball which rolled casually,
tauntingly, into the street...

at the exact moment of the
crash (a harsh, thund'rous

robert l. darden

impact of innocent, youthful
flesh against foreign craftsmanship),
nothing could be heard
over the screams and cries
of all who were in witness
but were unable to keep
the inevitable from being so…

as the sun faded completely away,
the tears were only beginning
to flow….

doomchildren.

look over there at "womanchild" :
sixteen-year-old sista with more
belly than food to go in it.
laughin'
('cause she just felt her belly move)
and cryin'
('cause she ain't got no food for the two of
      them…).

look over there at "manchild" :
little nigga sittin' on a stoop with
nowhere to be.
laughin'
(at sista-girl 'cause she's in a real jam this time)
and cryin'
('cause he knows he can't give her no food, even
      though he
gave her the belly…).

look all around for "helpthechild" :
you'll never find it.
not today. not tomorrow.
no one was there to warn the children.
no one was there to advise the children.
no one will be there to help the children raise
      the children…
'doomchildren' :
life, about to begin
through lives just barely begun
(yet already over)…

peace: my prayer.

patience. it's gonna take time to
 convince the mass (the fools who doubt)
 that you can do it,
even though it should only matter to
 you (and to the chosen few to whom you
 want it to matter).
always remember that the ones who
 really love you will be forever by your side,
 through the good and the bad…
constant reminder of your success and fame
 will be the smile on your face, and the
 pride which you feel.
each and every day belongs to you: take
 control, but take it easy. there's only
 so much one man can do. it's your turn
 for a miracle, so smile dammit!!!

you should know...

you should know that you're not the reason i am
    who i am you
  should know that about you i do not give a
    damn you should
  know that i made it this far on my own you
    should know that
i'm not 'fraid of bein' alone.
you should know that you're not the blood in
    my veins you should
  know 'though tears fell you're not cause for
    the stains you
  should know that i'm much stronger than
    you thought i could
  be you should know that without you i'm still
    'gon be me.

you should know that to me you don't mean a
    damn thing you
  should know that bruised hearts still have the
    power to sing you
  should know that you don't take up that
    much space in my head
  you should know that i enjoy the extra space
    in my bed.
you should know that each day carries on just
    the same you should
  know that i sometimes don't remember your
    name you should
  know that i'm lying when i say i don't miss
    you 'cause you should

robert l. darden

    know that i remember the first time i kissed
        you.

you should know that i blame you for all of this
        pain you should
    know that to see you i would walk through
        the rain you should
    know that i'll get by i'll be fine i'll survive you
        should know that
i've never been more alive.
you should know that some bridges are better
        once burned you
    should know that some lessons never truly
        get learned you
    should know that there's no need to make a
        big fuss 'cause you
    should know that it's over. everybody else
        does…

the quintessential acquired taste of a bone dipped in chocolate: a sexcapade...

...as i pick him up to carry him across the room, his heartbeat rallies the sound of any thunderstorm; as i lay him down on fresh, clean sheets, i realize that each thumping thud of his heart is echoed by my own heart—no other sounds occur...

...before i place the blindfold over his eyes, i gently kiss each of his pale eyelids three times, thus beginning my journey.

from there, i move to his forehead—still more kisses lead me to his ears. tiny, yet masculine ears. left. then right. from the lobe, i go to his neck, where i lavish the delicate skin which protects his throat. like a vampire having not partaken of any meal in this lifetime, but no harm do i bring my 'victim'. slowly. simply. lovingly. i move southward to his chest and i lick and caress the mounds of muscle that lay waiting there for me. i devote special attention to the proud, pink nipples, chewing and pulling the thick coating of hair that covers my playground; i imagine how they will look once they are adorned with small, thick silver hoops...

...downward still, i reach the valley of a navel designed to be drank from, and after seeing how far my tongue will go inside it, i shift further down into the thick, beautiful, sinfully aromatic wonderland of velvet forest, which encases a glory its own. (not wanting to neglect any parts not yet traveled, i temporarily bypass this treasure...) i begin to nibble on his inner thighs, causing him to tremble and squirm with delight. slowly (contentedly) i move to the queue of his derriere, seeking the rosy-pink pucker of his ass. (do i dare awake from this dream? no, no. not just yet.)...

...only after seemingly having caused his back to arch enough that his toes leave their mark on his forehead do i go back up to "la region d'irresistable": his cock is hard enough at this point to etch both our names in stone, and as i lick it from tip to base (and back), i feel his hands on the back of my head, and i know what it is that he is wanting me to do next. the entire length of his member disappears inside my mouth, and the muscles of my throat begin what can only be described as "the invisible massage". after several repetitions of this feat, he is ready to explode: i consume the spill from his eruption and as it trickles down my throat, he cries out my name, securing my mouth to his groin to insure that none of his seed is lost. upon the last gush from his fountain, i realize that i have neglected his mouth, so i slither back up his sweat-drenched, hairy body to unite his lips with mine, letting him taste all that i've just sampled…

…now, we are one forever, and i wrap my arms around him as we drift off into a slumber: mon ami mieux et moi, toujours je l'aime…

good night pooh-bear, love piglet.

i see him sitting there.
does he see me watching him?
has he seen me at all?
i walk by.
i toss him a glance.
oh, yeah, he saw me.
i try to play it cool.
he's just a man.
scratch that—
he's just a gorgeous fur-covered
bear-hunk of a man that i've
just got to flirt with.
i walk back over to where i was
sitting when i noticed him noticing me.
great! someone is talking to him!!
fuck!! there goes my chance to
meet one of the most—wait!
they've left and he's still sitting there!
if possible, he looks even cuter now!
i flash one of my best smiles, and
get up and walk by again.
this time the toss is of
a kiss on the air…
i'm hoping he'll follow me
to a quieter section of the bar.
two minutes. five minutes. ten minutes. damn.
i go back.
he's still sitting there, and,
of course, someone else
has noticed him, and has the
nerve to be chatting him up.

robert l. darden

fuck them for being all brave and friendly!!!
i retake my seat on the
single bar-stool, and again look
in his direction.
whoa! wait a minute! did he just
look at me?
all of a sudden i'm shy!
all of a sudden he's alone again!
all of a sudden i have no idea
what i should do!
all of a sudden
we're talking to one another!!!
sensory overload! sensory overload!
of all the times to practice restraint,
i fight the urge to run my hands
over his beautiful fur-covered chest.
you know what? fuck restraint!
grab a handful and see
where it goes from there…
suddenly i'm drunk—
intoxicated by mutual attraction and
a big splash of lust served on
two comfortably cautious smiles.
no glass. no ice. room temperature,
which at this moment, is rising.
dangerously…
we move to another spot, hoping
that walking around will allow
some blood to flow back to other
parts of our bodies.
no such luck.
and speaking of luck, here comes
another (uninvited) admirer.
the trio conversates; actually,

cursed blessings/blessed curses

they conversate as i try to figure out
subtle ways to make 3rd party relocate
and leave me alone with mr. p.
we go outside to cool off—yeah, all
three of us.
damn him!!
under the table (in way too subtle a manner),
i play with the leg of my intended prey
as we talk of the weather conditions of each
of our geographic homes—at least i think that's
what we talked about.
i was too busy staring at, and trying to re-gain
the attention of, the only reason
i was still at the bar,
not to mention the fact that
i was freezing.
but, so was he,
so back inside we went…
we're standing by the door and
the taller bear decides to leave.
hmmm, maybe there is a god…
we talk for a few minutes and
suddenly i'm shy again!
i can think of nothing to do or say!
what to do?
what to do?
what to d—
hey! are we kissing?
hot damn, are we kissing!
hella-woof can this man kiss!!!

the bar is about to close in
a few, and we're getting hungry.
after he drives me to my car

(gasp and swoon—how sweet is that!?),
we stop off for some "middle-of-the-
night-only-thing-open-happens-to-be-
on-the-way-convenience-nutrition-in-
the-form-of-a-square".
he's ahead of me by about four cars.
i begin to worry that—oh god!—i hope
he doesn't think i've changed my mind!
i hope he realizes that i'm still at the drive-thru,
and that he isn't thinking that i've changed my
      mind!
i hope that he doesn't think that i decided to go
home instead!
wait! why am i trippin'! i know he doesn't think
that i'd walk away from him—has he seen him?!
eventually, i get my food and off i go.
luckily, i know the location of the hotel
at which he's staying.
finally, i get there, all apologetic and shit.
thankfully, he waited for me.
we walk to the elevator.
does he know that i want to mount him?
(of course he knows—i'd already told him that
earlier—so much for subtlety, right?)
walking down the hallway to his 'den'
is a bit of an experience.
activities of a slightly deviant nature
are taking place right before our eyes.
fuck them for being shameless!
(besides, who am i to judge?) :{)~
suddenly, i realize that i'm walking with
one of the hottest guys of this
whole damned weekend.
confidence all across my face as we walk

cursed blessings/blessed curses

on past the relations, ovations, and fellations
on display.
he opens the door.
i pee (in the bathroom, of course).
we hug. we kiss.
he pees (bathroom, too—please, can i keep
 him?)
he gets comfortable.
i get more comfortable.
we're both a little too comfortable,
but that's not a bad thing.
we eat.
and talk. and watch tv.
and eat.
all the while, relaxing even more…
two hours later, we 'go to bed'.
roughly ten hours later, we get out of bed.
i think we even got some sleep.
yeah, as i recall, there was a little bit
of that, too…
he had warned me about his snoring.
told me that it would keep me awake.
it didn't.
it made me think him even cuter, if
that's possible.
yeah.
it was borderline perfect.
the best i've ever been made to feel in one
 evening.
damn him for making me want to
move to arizona!!!
i can still feel him in my arms.
never have i wanted to hold onto anything
or anyone more that i wanted to hold him

robert l. darden

when i got back to my own bed...

i saw him again the next night.
we talked. we kissed. but it didn't
compare to that first night.
did i mention that it was almost perfect?
anyway, he left the bar before i could say
"good-bye" or "until we meet again"—
i *will* see him again, won't i?
looks like there's a road-trip or
a flight in my future.
it's all good, and he's more than worth it.
until then, sweet dreams pooh-bear....

hallucinations.

screams
are held in suspension
wond'ring to themselves
if they are heard,
or if they'll fall like acid rain—
or if they'll soar like birds;

stars
are shining upside-down
with hopes of being seen—
just dangling in their pool of black,
looking down at what is green;

the sound of
silence
fills my head
with an annoying, inaudible hum—
it makes me wonder :
is this the end,
or is there more to come?

shattered equilibrium.

an ice cube,
sitting in the beginning
of what will
eventually become
a puddle,
is helpless against
the forces of nature,
just as humans are.
but the comparisons
stop there,
for once the ice
has melted,
it still has a use,
as well as
a purpose…

darkness.

i wonder, the reason that i'm here;
do i fit any part?
i wish that i
had some real purpose,
that i'd been made from the heart.

darkness falls in the middle of my day,
and makes me feel alone.
it washes away
all my thoughts,
and chills me to the bone.

i see eyes peering through the darkness;
their message is not clear.
it seems that they
are sad because
they know the end is near.

the perseverance of doubt.

six empty bottles.
serving as reminders of one's life;
their purpose fulfilled, they stand
only to be mocked
by the ones who worshipped them
moments ago.
although humiliated, they stand
tall and pray for the second chance
to bring temporary consolation and
mock-happiness to some poor,
ungrateful fool whose only
purpose is to "be"—
or maybe they are just standing:
standing only because they know
of nothing else to do.
who knows?

a moment of regret.

why did i bring you into this?
did you even want to be here?
what gives me the right to bring
   anyone into my personal hell?
why do i still feel the need to
   share it?
if i knew how, i'd shield you
   from all of this;
i'd give you the strength to
   walk away,
     pretending it never happened…
…even though i'd give anything
   to have you near me, i doubt
   that you'll ever be able to
   walk down this road that i am
   traveling:
but where will you go?
if you go this way, i'll be right
   beside you, holding your hand.
if you go that way, i can only give
   my heart as a companion, but…
…either way, you'll know that no
   one loves you as much as i do.
now or ever.
and i always will…

bitter...

sitting quietly
in a place
where time and money
are not your friends,
listening to
the sounds of nothing—
you begin to wonder:
when does this all end?...

suddenly, in spite of
all this darkness,
you realize
what is your fate:
by analyzing
your surroundings,
you find what leads
to all your hate...

on the road to insanity...

beautiful day;
i go for a walk.
lots of traffic.
but over the hum
of all the car engines,
i can still hear doors
being power-locked as i
walk in the direction of
cars sitting at traffic lights
and stop signs.
'shame that a man
can't walk down the street,
bare-handed,
and not be feared...
"he" thinks that i want to rob him.
"she" thinks that i want to rape her.
i don't need his money,
and if i *did* want her,
four locked doors would not
keep me from her...
besides: if anything,
i would take her money
so that i could take him out
to dinner and a movie...
but still, i get slapped
in the face by their
unintentionally rude displays of
exactly how far we have not come.
america—
home of the free,
land of the brave...(?)

storm.

lying alone in bed
in the middle of the afternoon,
simultaneously listening to
the thunder rolling outside,
and daydreaming about having
someone to hold on to, someone
to chase away all my fears…

…lightning strikes just
outside my window and jolts
me from my psuedo-slumber,
and as the rain begins to fall
from the sky, the tears begin
to fall from my eyes…

if it's me that you see...

hey, do you know me?
let me introduce myself:
i'm me. yes, me,
and no one else.
a role model is not
what i am, want, or need.
though i'd welcome compassion,
without it i'll breathe.
with ideas of my own,
alongside my own plans,
i live my own life—
on 'my own two' i stand,
so if it's me that you see
sitting atop a tree,
don't ask how, don't ask why—
i'm allowed 'cause i'm free.

if you think where i stand
makes me less of a man,
then forgive me for not
living life by your plans.
i'm a man of many moods.
i'm a man of many sides.
i'm a man's man, and yes,
i'm a man of great pride.
so if it's me that you see
goin' 'round, full of glee,
then i'm proud to announce
i'm just proud to be me.
young, beautiful, and free,
what more could there be?

robert l. darden

i'm lookin' down to cloud nine,
goin' places, you see?
so, if it's me that you see
sittin' sippin' some tea,
don't walk by, bounce on over,
grab a cup, and join me…

cette homme...

his eyes have always said "hello" to me
but, today it was almost as if
they didn't even see me,
for behind those eyes lurks
the vision of another:
the one who holds the key
to everything about him
that i adore.
such as his lips
(which i can only dream of kissing),
his arms
(which i can almost feel wrapping around me),
his hands
(which i wish i could hold in mine),
his body
(which i pray i'll someday be allowed to
    caress...)...
but today, those same eyes and hands say
"good-bye"
as those lips say
"i'm sorry",
and that body turns to walk away from me,
taking him home to the other one,
to the one with whom he wants to be:
the one with whom he belongs...

...as i view this
(over and over in my mind),
tears begin to flow from
my own eyes,
and i cry myself to sleep,

robert l. darden

knowing that he and i
will always (only) be friends.
it just doesn't seem to be enough. damn!

mosaique.

a shadow played with me for a while,
but that was an awkward day.
i could neither make him frown nor smile,
so i turned and walked away.

birds were flying overhead;
now they're on the ground,
waiting for people to toss some bread,
but it costs too much per pound.

golden spheres consume the page,
yet it still appears plain.
roses throw a fit of rage
amid violets dancing in pain.

dogs run through a field of grass;
flowers look up to the sky:
there were thousands of questions in my past,
but now all i ask is "why?"…

deux hommes.

friends, indeed; lovers, not really; brothers,
    within and beneath the skin.
saw through the darkness, broke the silence, and
    opened up the door
to **sin**…
incoherent screams of passion; moans and
    shudders laced with lust;
implied emotions, never spoken, seasoned with
    a dash of trust…
much, much more than exploration—fantasy
    revealed, then carried out;
physical communication which left no room for
    fear or doubt…
upon crumpled sheets that smell of sweat, mixed
    with candles melting away,
bodies wracked with pain and pleasure, now
    sleep, where earlier, they did 'play'…

symphonique.

music.
it flows through the air,
invading the senses in a mysteriously
melodic manner:
somehow, it transports us to
places we never thought we
could go.

because of music,
we share a common bond;
within music,
we are one;
through music,
we can communicate
with the world…

the conductor raises his hands,
and thus begins the
symphony of life…

zero.

as time goes by
i realize that
i honestly have nothing:
i came from nothing,
with nothing, and
i shall go into nothing
with nothing.
i have never experienced true love.
i have yet to encounter true happiness.
in all, i do not even recognize true misery…
still i have nothing.
i grow tired of my nothing,
because my nothing
is difficult to carry around
from day to day…

harmony.

…just as there is more to life than being male or female, there is certainly much more than black and white, and the rainbow that is see has a lot more than seven 'colours'.

knowing who you are, where you're from, and where you stand are important, but knowing the person standing next to you is equally important…

…when you dream, dream in colour. but when you're awake, let your heart be blind. it does not matter to whom you choose to give your love, only that you do give love. reality is such a nice friend to have. you're gonna get back all that you give out…

…a few miles directly ahead, there's a place called "human unity"—
go there with me….

dragphuck!!!

big dick. lipstick.
high heels. big pecs.
butch fag in make-up:
which way do you sex?
do you like to 'do'?
would you rather be 'done'?
so you 'stick' to one method,
or could it be either one?
pull down your panties
and untuck that dick,
but leave on your heels—
i don't care if you kick!
take it like a man,
and scream like a whore.
on your way out,
get your bra off my floor…

bondage (light).

eyes that speak of lustful mayhem
    greet you and bring you through the door.
across the room, you're going to them,
    'though your feet don't touch the floor…
lips of ruby red caress you
    and fill you in on all that's new.
hands as strong as hell undress you—
    what in your god's name shall you do?
standing naked, so excited,
    can't remember your own name.
you give in to pleasures uninvited;
    your body's ready—you're glad you came…
relax and let this moment happen—
    how often are there times like this?
in the future when spirits dampen,
    you'll think back to this blazing kiss!
you may feel that you are dreaming
    'cause things like this just don't happen to
        you,
but all the while, your heart is screaming:
    "anything can happen if you want it to!!"

bondage (severe).

th' handcuffs slip, but you can't move, 'cause
    they're as tight as tight can be.
sooner or later, you'll find th' groove: one way or
    another, you'll submit to me…
as candlewax drips onto my skin, i scream your
    name in sheer delight:
through our pain, we've both met **sin**, and he's
    agreed to spend th' night…
th' whips cracks, and then you feet th' burn—it
    leaves a mark that begins to swell.
you'd think that by now you would have learned,
    but no, your ass is red as hell.
th' blindfold on your eyes is tightened—all your
    senses run amuck.
th' level of arousal is severely heightened—my
    mind anticipates th' fuck…
after three hours, you're allowed release, and all
    about us is now wet;
you ignore my frantic cries of 'please!', for you're
    not finished. not just yet.
i reach up and grab your hair, your body jerks
    itself erect.
my tongue works you from here to there, no
    part of your person feels neglect.
you throw me down onto th' floor, which causes
    my own rush of blood.
neither of us can stand much more—in just a
    moment comes th' floor…
th' room becomes one with th' smell of lust;
    simultaneously, we both cry out.

cursed blessings/blessed curses

workin' our way to that final thrust, in sexual
    chorus our minds both shout.
as our bodies approach the utmost limits, we
    grind each other one more time.
this is a game not for th' timid—th' passion's
    intense. th' pain is sublime.

revolver.

labeled (by colour). judged (by tone).
dismissed (in spite of what we are: flesh and
    blood and bone).
unwanted (in society). unnatural (in thought).
evolved (from apes in theory, but that theory is
    not bought).
thankfully, times are changin', gettin' better in
    every way,
and even though it's goin' slowly, we'll take it
    (day by day)…

the sadist and the masochist.

a strap of black leather
with a buckle of brass
repeatedly lashes
across one partner's ass.

a lit cigarette,
the tip all aflame,
presses into one's skin
in this painful love-game.

wrist-straps and ice cubes.
chains, spikes, and whips.
the pulling of hair.
the biting of lips.

teeth grinding in agony
of torture *so* sweet.
bodies drenched in sweat
from their heads to their feet.

one partner is laughing
while the other one cries:
hands wrapped around throat,
tears of lust in the eyes.

one lover, the master.
the other, the slave.
they give and take orders
for the pain they both crave!

ego-trip (harsh/crude).

wrap your legs behind your ears and show me
    that you love me.
do you prefer bein' on your back or would you
    rather be above me?
tell me what you want from me—you know that
    i will please you:
i'll get some oil and heat it up, then rub you
    down and squeeze you.
tie me up and make me beg; don't worry, you
    can't hurt me.
and when you're done, i'll do the same, but i
    can't promise mercy…

close your eyes and count to ten—do you feel
    any better?
i'll tease you, then you'll tease me, but i bet i
    make you wetter!
i can unlock all you've got hidden and all you
    keep undercover.
with me, nothing is forbidden. you'll never find
    a more perfect lover!!

crowded solitaire.

petals
from one dozen
red roses,
scattered
about
the floor…

a lonely, confused,
barefoot man
walks across
the floor, a floor
which is covered
with the long,
thorn-laden stems
that were once
attached to those roses:
within his pain,
he realizes that
he is loved.

ma facade.

unspoken, rehearsed dialogue
runs through my head
waiting for the proper moment
at which to reveal itself,
as the thought of suicide
encircles and mocks
every serious thought
that manifests itself,
and once satisfied of feeding
off my fear and
total lack of courage,
it withers away and mocks
my entire existence until
only sleep can send it away from me…

defying all logic,
i continue to hide
behind the facade of
the happy, untroubled, secure,
lovable fool that
everyone expects me to be:

if they only knew ½ of
the evil that lurks in
the mind of one such as i…

pain.

pain—
in my head
in my heart
deep, deep within
why do i constantly
   allow myself to
   fall for the ones
   who are not
equipped/prepared/willing/able
   to give me all that
   i am wanting to
   give them?
it never fails—
i see them
and everything's o.k.
the things which
   need to be discussed
   are avoided, and then
   we go our separate ways
and the pain returns
the same sweet, deep,
   beautifully agonizing pain
   which carries me through
   my existence.
pain (…)

requiem d'amour?

can you hear me?
    as i tell you my story, i wonder whether or
        not you hear all that i
  say to you…
can you see me?
    as i stand before you, it feels as though you
        look right through me,
  if you look my way at all…
can you feel me?
    as i hold you in my arms, i sense that you are
        somewhere far, far,
  away…
speak to me; look at me; touch me.

although i'd be lost without you, i somehow feel
    lost
  when i'm with you:
are you there?
give me some indication that you and i are one,
or, at least, that we were at some point in the
        past…

seeing that you do not know me...

how exactly could you know me?
have we yet been introduced?
was it you with whom i talked?
was it you that i seduced?
have i told you of my struggles?
have i told you of my strife?
exactly when did i invite you, then,
to welcome yourself into my life?
why then do you feel the need
to talk to me as though a friend?
do you know of my beginning?
will you contribute to my end?
do i dare decide to trust you,
though i know not from whence you came?
will you answer when i call you?
do you even know my name?
seeing that you do not know me,
why before me do you stand?
do you want something that i have?
is my friendship in demand?
what is it which ties you to me?
is it something from my past?
do you know something about me?
do i even dare to ask?
are you trying to protect me?
is that what you've been sent to do?
well, to try and put it oh-so gently,
i don't want you, don't need you, don't even know you!
seeing that you do not know me,
there's nothing you can do for me.
i can take care of my damn self,
so this is the end—let me be!

je suis voici!

i heard that you knew somebody i know—
that doesn't mean that you know me, though!

so you've got more money, and you've got *the*
        car—
you think that i'm wanting to be what you are?

i'm sorry! no thank you! i'm content being me,
'cause i'm much better at it than you'd ever be!!!

a chance for change.

the only limits you should go by
are the ones you set for yourself.
do the things which give you pleasure.
live for you and no one else.
if you took the time to feel it,
take the time to let it be;
when the heart and mind are open,
soul and body can then be free.
when the feelings you're feeling
go against what you have learned,
maybe the books from which you learned
these things should all be found and burned…
words and thoughts from someone 'other'
contribute nothing to the taste
of the entree called compassion
which in front of you is placed.
you're the one who has to deal with
all the things going on inside.
what you need to do is draw a picture
and colour it in with pride…

hug.

the hug my best friend gave me on graduation
    night…
the hug i got form a friend on the last night of
    one special summer…
the hug that took all night…
the hug i didn't know was a hug…
the hug that only happens in my head…
the hug that ended with a kiss…
the hug that ended with much more than a
    kiss…
the hug that was just another hug…
the hug i gave to someone who needed a hug…
the hug that was more than a hug should be…
the hug that said "i'm sorry"…
the hug that said "i'll miss you"…
the hug that lasted longer than a day…
the hug that i give myself…
the hug that i'm sending to you right now…
the first hug…
the last hug…
all the hugs to come…

cast away your thoughts of loving me.

you smile as though you know me,
though your hist'ry i know not;
but i know enough 'bout you t' know
my attention's all you've got.
was there a plan on your behalf
to make me smile, or even laugh?
cast away your thoughts of loving me—
i refuse to walk that path…

the dance you dance is danced alone;
the song i sing ain't in your key;
though we're both on stage, and we both had lines,
all of yours were soliloquy.
it's not that i think i'm better than you,
just that i know that i deserve more.
cast away your thoughts of loving me—
move to the other side of the door…

take one last look at what you'll be missing:
see these lips you won't be kissing?
remember the swing of my hips as i walk,
but close your mouth baby, 'cause people do
      talk.
though i know that you want me like no one
      before,
all you want is some ass, and i offer much more.
cast away your thoughts of loving me—
my ship's afloat. you're still ashore…

cocky misguidance.

i have the strangest feeling that you want to rape
        me,
but rather than causing me worry, it causes me
to contemplate how much i want you to.
and how much i don't think you can…
you know how much i want to fuck you, and it's
obvious that you need to be fucked:
ev'rything about you just screams it!
so, what're you gonna do?
put a gun to my head and force me to penetrate
        you?
if that's your plan, tell all my friends that i
wish to be cremated—
i find it very difficult to obtain erection when
at the verge of bullet-through-cranium.
believe-it-or-not, i'm not even that kinky—
i think…

j/k/m/a.

spook. nigger. jigaboo. coon.
as if i had no feelings, just like a cartoon.
fruit. pansy. fairy. queen.
and all those stigmas in between.
darkie. crow. worthless slave.
careless titles to take to the grave.
sissy. queer. flaming fag.
choose your label from a paper bag…

not everyone must deal with such fate:
some people are just more convenient to hate.
but rather than simply letting it pass,
to my adversaries i say "just kiss my ass!"

oblivion.

somewhere
a child is running
through a rain-drenched
field of corn.
he knows not that today
is someone's last day
of existence—
he knows only that he
(himself)
can hear the sounds
of puddles being splashed—
and the cries
of cornstalks being
broken:
there is yellow
and green
(and water)
as far as
the ear can hear—
is this your heaven
or is this your hell?

je m'en fous!

i do not care anymore—
why should i?
it causes me only to be hurt
or severely disappointed.
i no longer possess the desire
to give a damn.
i will never again be let down.
no one has the right to see me cry.
no one has the power to cause me pain.
i am the only one who can make me feel
      anything, and
i no longer give a damn.
i do not care anymore:
je m'en fous!
(i don't give a damn!)
it hurts too much…

love '95.

can you stand here before me and say that you
 love me, when a few days
 ago you'd never heard of me?
if you *do* think you love me, here's a way you
 could prove it: get it up,
 get one on, get me off, *then* remove it.
i don't know where you've been, you don't know
 where i'm going;
 though we know where we're at, this takes
 more than just knowing.

when the night has gone, will you remember my
 name?
when the sun rises up, will it matter who came?
as the next day begins, will you recognize my
 face?
when the next night sets in, will it matter "whose
 place?"

don't play with my life:
here i am, get to know me!
when it comes down to love,
first tell me, then show me…

me times i.

at times i want to give it up and move on to
      another place,
but i'm afraid to take a seat beside an unfamiliar
      face.

at times i think of all the things i've never had
      the chance to learn,
but then i just crawl into bed and cry until my
      pillows burn.

at times i want to say "that's it!", and go on to
      another life—
foolishly i try to slit my wrist with the underside
      of a dull butterknife.

at times i want to scream and shout for all the
      things i can not see;
then i realize that they're still there, but unlike
      them, i am still me…

aural copulation.

close your eyes. you're all alone.
just you and a voice on your telephone.
confessing of things you never thought to tell:
your worries, they lessen. your senses, they gel.

your heart is racing, on fire with sin.
your fingers are tracing a path down your skin.
your ears hear the things that they've waited to
    hear:
no talk of commitment, so of course, there's no
    fear.

just when you think it can't get any better,
you're pushed passed your limit, and you begin
    to get wetter.
you welcome this pleasure. you writhe in your
    bed,
and right when it should happen, your damn
    phone goes dead!

you stare at the phone, wondering what went
    wrong.
no more is your pleasure. four bucks a minute,
    gone…
you *could* bring it back: dial the number again.
but are you willing to pay twice the price for one
    sin?!?…

le jeu d'amour.

love is a sometimes painful game, played
    between a pair,
who are not sure what's right or wrong, but just
    go on without a care.
pain is felt from time to time, but pain is only
    fair—
if there is always laughter, there is no real love
    there.
lovers tend to get upset by some of the habits of
    their mates,
but life's not always sunshine: you can't go uphill
    in skates…
in time we all may understand what it takes to
    share a life.
you don't have to have two golden rings to be a
    'husband' or a 'wife'.
you just need a love that's true and real. and a
    strong desire to live
with someone forever, 'til the end of time. learn
    to expect less than
  you give…
once you're there you'll feel it, maybe it will
    make you shout;
if what you've found is meant to be, then there
    shall be no doubt…

breakup!!

look at me and tell me how
you can say that you love me now,
then walk away to someone else
and offer him every part of yourself.
tell me how you can tell me lies
while looking directly into my eyes,
then have the nerve to scream and shout
when eventually i do 'find out'.
why do you use me like you do?
is it none for me but all for you?
do you have a heart? is it made of stone?
am i something to do? am i something you own?
do you keep me around for the occasional fix?
am i someone you use to just get your kicks?
do you think i get off on being abused?
do you actually think that i like being used?
do you think that without you i could not live?
that there's no one i'd rather my love to give?
every moment spent with you has been total
      waste:
there are so many other fruit which i've yet to
      taste.
i'm someone you deserved never to know, so
therefore i'm leaving—i've better places to go.

in summary...

what i'm looking for...
   someone to hold,
   someone to feel,
   someone to kiss,
   someone to look at,
   someone who'll look back,
   someone to love.
what i need...
   a partner,
   a codependent,
   a companion,
   a friend,
   a depth.
what i've found...
   confusion,
   complication/combustion,
   constant contamination
   (of decent intentions).
what i've got left...
   time (too much), and
   patience (not enough)....

everything.

everything that i am
is everything i should be.
it all depends on the focus
that i have within me.
everything that i am
and everything that i'll be
all rely on the efforts
that i put forth daily.
everything that i am
and all i've come to be,
all resulted from my
being true to just me.
everything that i am
and everything that is me
shows itself in the beauty
that is infinity…

everything that you are—
is it everything you should be?
that depends on your vision
of what you could be.
everything that you are
and everything that you'll be
all rely on those things
that you don't let kill thee.
everything that you are
and all you've come to be,
are right in front of your face,
but you must choose to see.
everything that you are
and everything that is you
shows itself in the glory
of all that is true…

Epilogue

I would just like to take this moment, here at the end, to thank and acknowledge all of those who, in one way or another, led to this collection, whether they know it or not. Some of their names may have changed at this point, but they (& I) know who they were/are: Mary Frances Dulworth, Natalie P. Albin, Vincent L. Harden, Selina White, Anthony R. Fox, Cameron & Rebecca White, Daniel L. Colouro, Michael R. Coffey, Jason P. Fleenor, Jeromy B. Neblett, the Chorale Students from Tennessee's Governor's School for the Arts from 1988, Dr. Raphael Bundage, Ken Patterson, Jamie Narviez, Hunter M. Moore, David L. Luffman, Abraham Perez, Damien L. Hardin, Jazzmyn, Mary Werth, Stephen Cole, Dr. George L. Mabry, Dr. Sharon Mabry, Bernard Crockrell, Dr. Thomas King, Kelly Wright, Allyn Phares, Deon Hunter, Phi Mu Alpha Sinfonia @ Austin Peay State University (too many individuals to name…), Thomas B. (TC) Smith, Jurgen Muller, Karla Arwood, Jason Norris, David Baldwin, Curtis Porter, Kerri Powers, Don Davidson, Wm. Jeffrey Riggle, D. Brian Baldwin, Mary (Diva) Trogdon, Kathy M. Hogan, Christy Vail, Rae Tummins, Lucinda Freeman, Michael Meise, and my sister's mother…

These are the people who, in no particular order, have influenced my writing, be it positively or negatively; if you feel I have omitted you, please acknowledge yourself, on my behalf, as you acknowledge my humanity—with all of its flaws…

Made in the USA
Columbia, SC
13 January 2025